YESTERDAY AND TODAY

YESTERDAY AND TODAY

Jack D Watford, MBE

'REMEMBER

your leaders, those who spoke to you the Word of God.

CONSIDER

the outcome of their life and imitate their faith.

JESUS CHRIST

is the same yesterday and today and forever.'

★ ★ ★

Hebrews 13:7-8

© Jack Watford 1995

First published 1995

British Library Cataloguing-in-Publication Data.
A Catalogue record for this book is available from the British Library.

ISBN 1 897987 13 7

Cover design by Matthew Slater

Printed and bound in Great Britain by Stanley L Hunt (Printers) Ltd, Midland Road, Rushden, Northants NN10 9UA

CONTENTS

To
MIRA
my wife, whose loving support
over more than fifty four years
has made all the difference

FOREWORD

Ever since I first attended Watford Crusader Class as a boy of ten I have had a growing affection and admiration for the Crusader movement. Through its help and teaching I learnt to memorise the Scriptures and in its leaders I found my early Christian heroes. Some like Ken Savage and Bill Fryer were killed in the War; others have lived on to continue influencing young lives through Crusaders or in the ordained ministry.

In those early days Jack Watford was just a name - to be revered for his work as the General Secretary, though also because of his excellent choice of surname. Now, as a neighbour and friend, Jack has given me the inestimable honour of writing a brief foreword to his history of the Crusaders' Union.

It is a gripping story and makes irresistible reading. The story of the movement's growth from earliest beginnings to the strength and maturity of the present day is told with Jack Watford's unmistakable story-telling skill. It is a story to inspire and to evoke a heart-felt sense of thanksgiving to God for what He has done through what began as a loose-knit organisation of dedicated lay Christians with a love for the Gospel, a concern for young people and a determination to do nothing other than keep 'looking to Jesus'. It is a story well told and well worth telling.

John St Albans

AUTHOR'S PREFACE

Scripture tells us there are some things best forgotten, but there are others in which memory has an important part to play. Again and again the Children of Israel were told to remember the wonder of their deliverance from Egypt and God's faithfulness in bringing them ultimately into the promised land.

Here on a smaller canvas is a word picture which also tells of God's faithfulness in a modern setting. I hope it will bring pleasure to older readers as they remember with gratitude all that membership of Crusaders meant to them in earlier years. I also hope it will encourage those who are now, or soon will be, active in continuing the work started so long ago. In many respects the challenge which they face today is far greater than it has ever been, but the calling is the same and so too are the resources available. May this record also serve to stimulate prayerful support from those of us no longer in the front line.

And now I have some debts of gratitude to pay, first of all to John Taylor, Bishop of St Albans, for so willingly contributing the Foreword, and also for the way he supports Crusaders at every opportunity. Then to Ernie Addicott who, when Director, asked me to have a go at writing a history of Crusaders, and for his encouragement after reading the first 'sample' chapters. I hope he will not be disappointed with the final outcome.

Next, my thanks to Heather Keep, Assistant Director, for all her expert help and wise guidance in dealing with such practical matters as layout, illustrations, printing and final production. Her co-operation has been invaluable.

Last, but far from least, is my gratitude to three old friends whose fellowship in Crusaders extends over very many years. Without going into detail, there came a time when the possibility of the history being printed and published seemed very remote. Geoffrey Roberts, learning of the impasse, asked to see the manuscript and having read it, felt concern to see it published. He shared his concern with Colin Walker and Dennis Lowden, and together they agreed to offer help in a very positive way.

Geoffrey, Colin and Dennis had all been leaders of the Golders Green Class, together with Ernest Bartlett. Ernest had established a Stewardship Trust and on his death, his three co-leaders as trustees, had the responsibility of administering the Trust to a conclusion. When donating a considerable sum to Crusaders, the trustees earmarked a portion of it towards the cost of publication of the history. It made all the difference and you will understand why no words that I can find will express adequately my gratitude for such generous and practical support.

Finally, I feel I should offer an apology because from time to time I found myself involved personally in the narrative, not out of any desire for publicity, but simply because, in some instances, I was participating in the activity recorded. Also in one or two places I have included a personal observation on a particular matter. Please be understanding and forgiving for, having been closely connected with Crusaders since 1919, forty years of which were at Headquarters, I would have found it hard to have written myself out of the narrative completely.

It is my sincere hope you will enjoy what you read and that it will have the effect of giving glory to God, knowing full well that: "apart from Me you can do nothing", John 15:5.

1

AN OPEN DOOR

"How is it that you boys are not at Sunday School?" To the small group of boys, the tall gentleman's polite enquiry appeared perfectly reasonable, for the year was 1900 when, as a matter of course, all boys and girls were expected to attend afternoon Sunday School organised by the various churches to which their respective families belonged.

"We don't like it, Sir," was the simple but clearly genuine reply to the enquiry. "What a pity" said the gentleman, and then added with a smile "if I were to start a Bible Class specially for you, would you like to come?" They said they would and the following Sunday afternoon at 3 o'clock, four boys arrived at the open door of No 71 Crouch Hill in Crouch End, North London, where Albert C Kestin was waiting hopefully and prayerfully to receive them.

Little did he realise at the time that, in fact, God was opening a door of opportunity to meet a developing need which, in the years to come would involve thousands of young folk who, having attended Sunday School for a while, would re-echo the words of that small group of boys in Crouch End, "We don't like it, Sir," and in more recent days, many thousands more for whom Sunday School or its equivalent, would not even be considered.

Albert Kestin was a young missionary with the Church Missionary Society in India and was enjoying his first furlough after working in Calcutta. He had decided that before returning to India he would seek ordination and accordingly was attending St John's Theological College in Highbury, North London, and living temporarily in nearby Crouch End, in the home of a Mr and Mrs W P Saffery.

They were a godly couple and it was they who first felt concern at having seen, on several occasions, a group of boys evidently out for a walk on a Sunday afternoon when clearly they would normally have been in Sunday School. The Safferys had made it a matter for prayer and, in due course, they shared their concern with their lodger and suggested he should do something about it. "What do you want me to do?" he had enquired. Their reply was a challenge, "Why don't you start a Bible Class for them here in our drawing room?"

At the time it seemed an outrageous suggestion, surely the local church folk would be horrified; he would undoubtedly be accused of 'sheep stealing', besides the youngsters might belong to different denominations, which in those days were clearly recognised and strictly observed by all concerned - the word 'ecumenical' had not been invented! Mrs Saffery's simple logic demolished all argument, "You are a missionary and here is a need!"

So it was that in the Spring of 1900 Albert Kestin, with mission in mind, set out for a walk on that Sunday afternoon, praying as he went that he might meet the boys in question, and might have the help and guidance of God in speaking to them. In later years he could say with Abraham's servant of old, "Blessed be the Lord God.... I being in the way, the Lord led me."

Of course there was opposition; in those days there were those who thought he was foolish to contemplate holding a Bible Class outside the auspices of the various denominations; to them it didn't make sense and anyway seemed basically wrong. Today we can recall, perhaps with justifiable amusement, the fact that four boys attended their first meeting on Sunday the first of April! If Kestin could be called a fool then it was for Christ's sake, and he was in good company (1 Cor 4:10).

At the time the possibility of founding a movement never arose, the very idea would have seemed preposterous; it was simply a question of responding to a small local problem peculiar to Crouch End; however, as the weeks went by, more and more boys joined the Class, and Mr Kestin felt a need for a partner to share in the leadership. This need was met in the person of Herbert Bevington, a young, like-minded friend who recognised the value of what was being done and who, during a church service, felt constrained to offer to help. His offer came as an answer to prayer and was gratefully accepted, but little did he guess what lay ahead, how the rest of his long life would be affected or how greatly he would be involved in the development of the movement.

It gradually became clear that what initially had been a temporary measure to meet a local need, now looked like becoming a permanency, in which case a suitable title seemed desirable. This need was brought to a head when it was decided to print an invitation card which members could give to any of their friends who were not attending a Sunday School. One day when looking through a book, Mr Kestin came across an illustration of a mediaeval Crusader standing with his hands resting on his sword; beneath the picture was the motto "Be Strong". The more he considered the picture the stronger came the conviction that here was not only the illustration required for the invitation card, but also the answer to his need for a title. Was he not engaged in a

Albert C Kestin, the Founder

Where it all started in Crouch End, North London

Crouch End Crusaders in 1901

'crusade' with the aim of winning the 'holy land' of boyhood, which the infidel Satan was seeking to possess? And so Albert Kestin obtained the title he was seeking, namely 'The Crouch End Crusaders' Bible Class', little realising how important the description was to become in the years that lay ahead. Incidentally, he also secured the block of the picture for his invitation card which, at the time, seemed just as important as the title!

With the theological course at St John's College completed successfully, ordination followed and the time came for the now Reverend Albert Kestin to return to Calcutta. He formally handed over the leadership of the Crusader Class to Herbert Bevington and sailed for India in September 1901. Notwithstanding careful observance of the rule to admit to the group only those boys not attending a Sunday School, the numbers increased steadily until it became clear that the drawing room of 71 Crouch Hill had reached saturation point. So it was that in 1902 a move was made to the large dining hall of Oakfield School in nearby Haslemere Road.

While Crouch End has the undoubted right to be recognised as the first Crusader Class, Mr and Mrs Saffery were not the only ones who had felt concern at the number of boys not attending Sunday School.

The obvious success of the group in Crouch End prompted other Christian men to consider, and prayerfully seek the guidance of God, as to whether they too should respond to the challenge. They found in Herbert Bevington a warm-hearted friend who shared his experiences and his methods with infectious enthusiasm. Soon there were Crusader Classes in High Barnet, Muswell Hill, Stroud Green, Richmond and Clapham. Then in 1904, Mr Bevington moved to the South Coast and immediately formed the Brighton and Hove Class which he led with such zeal that within twelve months he had a membership of 100 boys! There were also Classes at Hull, Ealing, Chiswick and Wandsworth.

By 1906 there were eleven independent groups, and others were being planned. There was still no Union although, thanks to the enthusiasm of Herbert Bevington, Classes were kept in touch with each other by means of a weekly 'Returns Sheet' which not only listed the attendance numbers of each group on the previous Sunday, but also included requests for prayer, together with news of the possible formation of new groups.

Although there was no formal federation there was an ever deepening sense among the leadership of belonging to each other in an exciting pioneering venture which was being signally blessed by God. Leaders felt an exhilarating freedom to develop their Classes in their own way, a freedom which was not often possible under the auspices of church or chapel where the wishes of clergy and ministers would have to be taken into account, and where it would be necessary to fit in with other church interests and activities.

With the opening of the new century it seemed that God was doing something unusual to meet an unusual need and in this situation the message to the church in Philadelphia appeared wholly relevant: "I know your works. Behold, I have set before you an open door" (Rev 3:8).

2
AN OPEN FIELD

Albert Kestin had returned to what was called the mission field which, in those days, meant overseas; but he knew that the field was really 'all the world' including Britain and he rejoiced greatly as regular letters from Herbert Bevington told of the new groups which were being formed under the name 'Crusaders'.

When in 1906, Mr Bevington received the news that Mr Kestin would be returning from India, it seemed an ideal opportunity to arrange a meeting to welcome him home, to introduce him to all the leaders, and to bring him up-to-date with the progress of the work. So it was that on 29th March 1906, almost 6 years to the day since those four boys arrived for the first time at 71 Crouch Hill, the Leaders of eleven Crusader Classes, with a total membership of some 600 boys, met together at Sion College, situated on the Victoria Embankment, close to Blackfriars Bridge in London.

The minutes of that meeting, recorded in delightfully clear copperplate lettering, tell us that after appointing a chairman, three of those present were commended to God in prayer because they 'would shortly be going abroad for missionary work' - they were moving from one mission field to another.

Mr Bevington 'then briefly outlined the rise and progress of the work since its inception.... and suggested that the time was now ripe for the formation of a central organisation together with a fund to meet the expenses'. Leaders would be responsible for their own Classes 'it being understood that the whole Bible be taught as the Word of God, and a keen evangelical and protestant spirit maintained, the Classes remaining unsectarian and working as far as possible in harmony with all denominations and local churches'.

The response was immediate and unanimous and by the time the meeting was over, 'Crusaders' had been officially born, a Committee of five had been chosen, and it was agreed that each group would make an annual contribution of 2s 6d (12p in today's currency!) for each ten members on the roll; the weekly 'Returns Sheet' would continue to be circulated, and the Rev A C Kestin was elected as the movement's first President. It had been a momentous occasion.

Herbert Bevington, whose zeal established the movement

Muswell Hill Crusaders in 1909

Finchley Crusaders in 1910

Ever since that first Sunday six years previously, the prayerful interest and support of Mr and Mrs Saffery had never ceased and now, once again, they were ready to provide for an evident need. A room in their house on Crouch Hill was gladly set aside as an office where all the secretarial work could be dealt with and records maintained. It could fairly be regarded as the movement's first official Headquarters.

Strangely enough, at first no-one felt the need for a formal title, the name 'Crusaders' seemed quite sufficient, but by 1907 something a little more explicit was required and 'The Crusaders' Union of Bible Classes' was chosen or 'The Crusaders' Union' for short.

It also seemed advisable to define the purpose of the movement and early records reveal that: 'It has as its object, the advancement of Christ's Kingdom amongst public and private schoolboys, with the promotion of all that tends towards a true Christian manliness'.

It may not be easy for those born in post-war Britain to understand the limiting of the objective to 'public and private schoolboys' but, at the time, social structures were such that it was a perfectly reasonable decision; it had quickly become evident that those were the boys for whom Sunday School was losing its appeal, so the aim was to meet that need. There had never been any desire to compete with the work of the churches which appeared at the time to be dealing satisfactorily with the needs of most boys and girls generally; the last thing Leaders desired was to antagonise their local churches by indiscriminate recruiting. The social changes in post-war Britain saw the end of the need to retain any restriction on membership. In this connection it should be mentioned that some groups happily include members with a Roman Catholic background.

In October 1907, a small prospectus was printed which indicated the aims and methods of the movement, and about that time Leaders expressed a desire for a distinctive badge of membership which could be worn by all concerned. The matter was discussed fully at the annual meeting of Leaders in that year and the relevant minute makes somewhat quaint reading. A Leader 'moved that it was desirable that Crusaders should have some distinctive colours or badge or symbol whereby they might know one another'. The motion was seconded and an animated discussion ensued. The proposition which found most favour was 'that there should be a small symbol or sign which could be worn on a watch chain, etc and would be easily recognised by Crusaders but convey nothing to outsiders'! Mr S de J Lenfestey, a Leader of the group at Blackheath, had an artistically minded brother who was also very knowledgeable in respect of armorial bearings and he kindly agreed to have a go at producing something suitable. The name 'Crusaders' turned his thoughts to knights in armour and then to the sixth chapter of the letter to the Ephesians where St Paul refers to the Christian's armour. With the Shield of Faith as background, Mr Lenfestey added the Cross of Christ, the Sword of the Spirit, the Helmet of Salvation and the Crown of Righteousness. His draft met with instant approval and, all down the years, the wearing of the badge has meant far more than a mere indication of membership for, in addition, it was often a sign of the wearer's greater allegiance; at first when at school and later in the adult world. Deep and lasting friendships have frequently been established between complete strangers as a result of recognising the small badge in the wearer's buttonhole.

So that the badge could also be used on publications, letter headings and also embossed in gold on the cover of Bibles, it was felt that an acceptable crest could be created by the addition of a scroll with a motto in Greek, as was the custom in those days. Albert Kestin suggested as a motto the words from Hebrews 12:2 'Looking unto Jesus'. It was an inspired proposal encapsulating, as it did in three short words, the aim and object of the movement. Thus it was that by 1908, the desire for an official emblem had been fully met and, since then, the badge has been worn by thousands upon thousands to be recognised and respected by Christians the world over. So much for the original suggestion that it should 'convey nothing to outsiders'!

"The field is the world," said Jesus in one of His parables, and The Crusaders' Union has never ceased to regard itself as a missionary society working in an increasingly needy corner of that field. In those early days of its formation, many church-going parents were becoming concerned at their sons' reluctance to attend Sunday School and were delighted to find an alternative which appeared to capture their allegiance in a quite remarkable way. They were intrigued to see the pleasure, not to say pride, with which the badge - presented after ten consecutive attendances - was being worn and, in addition, the surprising readiness to set off for Crusaders in good time where previously there had to be unwelcome reminders and persuasions.

At times this strong allegiance became somewhat embarrassing when, for example, the occasional Sunday visit to tea with Grandma, had to be delayed until 4 o'clock because Tom, Dick or Harry were determined not to miss Crusaders.... even once!

The Minutes of the second Conference of Leaders on 20th March 1907 include a report on the previous twelve months, given by Mr Bevington as Hon General Secretary. This contained the encouraging news that: 'the number of Crusader Classes had increased from 11 to 19 and the membership from 600 to well over 1,000.... it was hoped to open 3 more branches in the next month'.

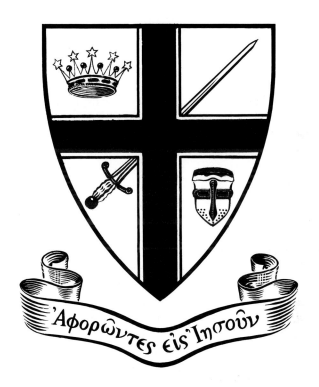

3

AN OPEN INFORMALITY

During the early years of the 20th century, religion was generally regarded, particularly among the middle class, as a matter for serious observance and pious conformity. Church members and their families took it for granted that they would attend Sunday morning worship, and for many, Sunday evening too. Sunday afternoon for adults was the time to read books of a serious nature, while the maid did the washing-up after Sunday dinner prior to having the afternoon off. The master, as he was called, might take a short walk, but that would be the extent of any 'sporting' activity.

No shopkeeper would dream of opening his shop on a Sunday and any traffic, horse-drawn of course, would be a rarity - all was peace and quiet! So for most youngsters Sunday was a deadly dull day made even less attractive for boys by their having to wear their 'Sunday best' suits which usually included a thoroughly uncomfortable stiffly starched 'Eton' collar, the edges of which, when slightly worn, felt more like rough sandpaper; bad enough in winter, unbearable in summer - I write with feeling!

Sunday school was often 'stiff and starchy' too; small wonder that boys were attracted to something so completely different - the reverent but cheerful informality which characterised the Crusader Class.

A Leader would be at the entrance of the meeting place to greet each boy with a friendly smile and a warm 'Crusader' handshake. The significance of which had to be learnt. It simply consisted of linking the little finger with that of the person with whom one was shaking hands!

Inside the meeting place would be a group of boys examining the Notice Board on which, apart from items of local interest, would be the Returns Sheet indicating the number which attended each Crusader Class the previous Sunday and the total for the whole Union. The aim of each Class was to grow and so climb higher and higher up the list.

Leaders took care to post their Returns card on their way home from Class - the postage was a halfpenny in the old currency - and the card reached Headquarters in time for the next Returns Sheet to be prepared and circulated to all Classes for display the following Sunday; in those days the postal service was both reliable and cheap. Included with the Returns Sheet would be Union news so that all were kept fully informed of progress and future plans, and there were also requests for prayer. This regular weekly link played a very important part in binding the Union together as a fellowship; unfortunately cost and deterioration of the postal service ultimately made it impossible to continue.

Promptly at 3 o'clock one of the Leaders would take his seat as 'chairman' behind a small table and the boys would settle down in the rows of chairs opposite him. The first item was usually a hymn although some Classes had their own 'Opening Chorus', one version of which went as follows:

> 'God bless our Crusaders,
> Bless each Class, we pray
> May Thy Word find entrance,
> In each heart today.
> Let Thy Holy Spirit
> With each one now deal,
> And with power in this hour
> Christ reveal.
>
> Lord, we wait before Thee,
> Wait Thy word to hear,
> Take Thy yoke upon us,
> And Thy burden bear;
> So through every speaker
> May we hear Thee say:
> "Come and see, go and tell,"
> Then obey.'

What followed was always bright and thoroughly relevant to a boy's experience – a short prayer, a Scripture reading with a brief explanation, often taken by a senior boy; a suitable hymn or two but, in addition, a selection of choruses usually chosen by the boys themselves. Choruses were tremendously popular, they were brief, most expressed a Scriptural truth or injunction, sometimes they were actual words of Scripture, and each was set to a good tune which could be learnt very easily.

In the report of that first Leaders' Conference of 1906, reference was made to the desirability of preparing a Chorus Book 'as soon as possible' and one of those present, a gifted musician named Williams Perkins, was given the job.

He clearly got to work at once for included in the Financial Report a year later are the words: 'Against the debit balance of £2 10s 5d must be set the 1,000 Chorus Books in stock'.

It would be hard to exaggerate what choruses have meant to thousands of Crusaders all down the years, fixing, as they did, a precious Scriptural truth in both mind and heart which often became more and more meaningful in the rough and tumble of adult life. This was particularly true during two World Wars; for these were occasions when by simply whistling the tune of a chorus in a barrack hut or on board ship, many found a fellow Christian at a time when Christian fellowship made such a difference when in a strange environment, separated from home and loved ones and when the future appeared dark and dangerous.

A typical Crusader meeting in the early 50's – the front row is never very popular!

There was also comfort in a chorus such as:

> *'All glory be to Jesus*
> *The sinner's only Saviour,*
> *Whose precious blood for sin atones*
> *And blots it out for ever.*
> *To know Him is to love Him,*
> *To trust Him is to prove Him,*
> *And those He saves*
> *He ne'er forsakes*
> *No never - never - never.'*

There was no set pattern for a Crusader meeting, which made possible that vital ingredient called variety, but there would always be a slot for 'Notices' which might often have been justifiably renamed 'Humorous Interlude'. Fun and laughter have always had a place in any Crusader gathering, not because it was purposely intended or staged but because joy is part of our Christian heritage and it wells up at appropriate times.

The Notices would include news of future plans such as games evenings or outings. There would be a welcome for any new members, perhaps the presentation of a badge and, when appropriate, reference to some special Union event; for example on 13th January 1908, the first Annual Rally of Crusaders was held in the Memorial Hall, Farringdon Street, near Ludgate Circus in London. It was attended by some 500 Crusaders from 21 different Classes and for the first time members had a visual awareness of the size of the movement to which they belonged.

Towards the end of the hour-long Class, one of the Leaders, or a visiting speaker, would give a short Bible-based talk and proceedings would usually conclude with a hymn or chorus and a prayer. It might seem that all this represented nothing very unusual but, in fact, many boys returned home with a strangely satisfying feeling of inner well-being hard to define and, at their age, impossible to explain. They weren't to know that much prayer had been made by the Leaders in which, more often than not, each boy had been thought about and remembered by name. They weren't to understand until later the reality of Christ's presence in the person of the Holy Spirit, nor the power and authority of the Scriptures - the truth which sets free.

Herbert Bevington on one occasion was greatly moved overhearing two of his members discussing his Class at Finchley, when one said to the other, "You know at Crusaders they care for a chap."

4

AN IMPORTANT LINK

Towards the end of the 19th Century, it was the custom of many middle class families to visit a fashionable seaside resort during the summer holidays, often going to the same place year after year. The children would play on the beach and would meet their friends from previous visits.

In 1868 a young office worker named Josiah Spiers was also taking his holiday by the sea. He had recently been greatly impressed by the unusually informal methods used by an American evangelist at meetings organised for children and he had commenced meetings of his own in Islington in North London, where a similar informality was proving equally popular with the local children.

Josiah Spiers had chosen Llandudno on the North coast of Wales for his holiday and as he watched the children playing on the beach, he noticed some were using pebbles and seaweed to construct a garden. It was typical of the man that soon he had several of the children helping him construct the text 'God is love'. By the time it was finished quite a crowd had gathered round and they readily accepted his offer to tell them a story.

In the previous May, Josiah Spiers and his friend Tom Bishop had decided to call their Islington meeting the 'Children's Special Service Mission' and in the years that followed more and more banners, with the letters 'CSSM' on them could be seen on the beaches of holiday resorts around the coast of Britain during July and August. This meant that Christian men and women - many of them university students - were holding a daily beach service for children, followed by all kinds of happy activities.

One of the many ways in which, in early days, the CSSM helped Crusaders was in connection with a magazine. The desirability of having a regular periodical was recognised from the start, but the cost of a production which at first would have only a limited circulation, posed a problem. However the Minutes of that first meeting of Leaders in 1906 record the following: 'The question of having our own magazine was introduced and on the suggestion of the General Secretary the meeting decided to adopt 'Our Boys Magazine' and to endeavour to arrange for a special cover, with extra sheets added for the printing of purely Crusaders' news'.

'Our Boys Magazine' was produced by the CSSM and contained excellent material including serial stories. I well recall being puzzled in 1919 when I purchased my first copy and discovered that I seemed to have two magazines in one, the reason for which was beyond my youthful understanding. In fact it had proved possible to have extra pages of Crusader material bound in and also to have our own Crusader cover. Some of those serial stories were most exciting, particularly those written by J B Phillips who years later became famous for his modern translation of the New Testament epistles under the title 'Letters to Young Churches'.

During the years that followed, the Crusader editorial pen was held by ten different people until in 1931 the mantle of Hon Editor fell on Cecil J Allen, for many years a Leader of the High Barnet Class. He worked for what was then the Great Eastern Railway, (later incorporated in the London and North

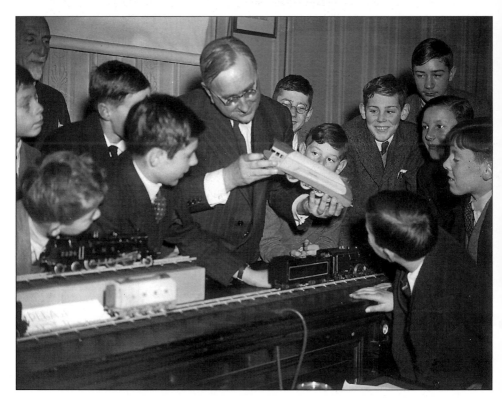

High Barnet Crusaders enjoy Cecil Allen's model railway

Magazines have played an important part down the years

Eastern Railway) and was responsible for the quality of steel used in the production of railway lines.   His knowledge of everything connected with railways was encyclopaedic and his many journeys, necessitated by his work, gave him considerable time to write, and he was a very gifted writer.   When his autobiography 'Two Million Miles of Train Travel' was published, 'The Guardian' newspaper gave it an enthusiastic review referring to Cecil Allen as one 'who has dominated the world of railway journalism almost since the day in 1908 when he began his monthly articles on railway practice and performance'.   No doubt some of his books, more than forty in all, may still be found in the libraries of Britain. Cecil Allen was not content with an inset and very soon 'The Crusaders' Magazine' was a top quality independent production, read with enjoyment and profit by thousands of Crusaders.   Mr Allen quickly realised that much of what the magazine contained was over the heads of most junior members and he persuaded the gifted leader of the Leicester Evington Class - Wilfred White, to become 'The Junior Editor'.   It was a wise decision and an excellent choice, and for seven years, up to the outbreak of war, the juniors had several pages each month specially for themselves.   A glance at some of the old bound copies at Headquarters makes one realise how well they were catered for.

When the time came for Cecil Allen to retire as Editor, the Union was fortunate to have on the General Committee, Randle Manwaring, a Leader with considerable literary gifts, who, in more recent years, has had works of his own published. He wielded the editorial pen for five years and then handed it on to Bill Latham, a Leader of the Finchley Class and whose co-leader for a time was Cliff Richard.

Others who over the years have had a hand in editing the magazine include Brian Lilley, Graham Disbrey and Denis King.   In its day this monthly production helped to give the Union a sense of togetherness for, among other things, it was a regular reminder to the individual Crusader that he belonged to a movement far greater than his local group.   Alas the ever increasing cost of printing and distribution finally made continuance of the magazine economically impossible.   The Union was poorer for its demise, but today 'Link' magazine is produced for Leaders, Associates and Students.

5

AN OPEN BIBLE

'Faith comes by hearing, and hearing by the word of God' wrote St Paul in his letter to the Romans; and from the start Crusader Leaders made it their aim to instruct their members in the Scriptures so that they might become 'wise unto salvation through faith which is in Christ Jesus'. Therefore in addition to Bible based talks on Sundays, boys were encouraged to read a few verses of Scripture every day. Clearly some reading scheme was needed and help in this matter came once again from the CSSM. In the early days of that movement a young Sunday School teacher in Keswick had written telling how in an endeavour to encourage the girls in her class to read the Bible for themselves, she had prepared lists of suitable readings for the coming week which she distributed every Sunday, and the following Sunday they discussed what they had read. Because the method had proved so acceptable she suggested the CSSM should print and circulate a list of daily portions suitable for children so that others might enjoy a similar benefit.

Strangely enough in those days, it was not thought that children would wish to read the Bible for themselves and at first no action was taken but, thanks to the persistence of that Sunday School teacher, it was decided to try out the idea and in 1879 a card was produced containing a list of readings, it cost one penny and the purchaser automatically became a member of the 'Children's Scripture Union'. The Hon Secretary was T B Bishop, later to be closely associated with Crusaders; and so Class members were encouraged to join the Scripture Union and to read the appropriate passage of the Bible each day.

Mr Bishop had originally wanted three sets of readings for different age groups but his Committee decided that everyone should read the same daily passage, and this remained the case until about 1930. At that time I, among others, was assisting Jack Hoare in the leadership of our very large Junior Section of the Muswell Hill Class. He had come to the conclusion that the SU readings were too long and sometimes quite unsuitable for youngsters of eight to eleven years old. He discussed the matter with the CSSM who kindly agreed to print a card for Juniors provided he would plan the portions to be read in the coming year. I had just left school and had some time to spare, with the result that the job of selecting those portions fell on me! It's nice to have had a very small share in the SU saga. Now of course there are readings for all ages with helpful explanatory notes to match, and their use is world-wide.

Crusader 'Knighthood' Bibles, yesterday and today – usually awarded after 50 attendances

6

COME TO CRU CAMP

One of the many benefits enjoyed by young folk resulting from membership of a movement greater in numbers than could comprise a Church Sunday School, is the ability to provide activities of a kind and on a scale not normally possible in the local situation. So it was not long before consideration was being given by the founders to what was to become one of the most popular items in Crusaders' annual programme.

In the Minutes of the second Conference of Leaders in March 1907, we find the following:

'Summer Camp. The question of a camp for Crusaders during summer holidays was raised and, on the suggestion of Mr Lenfestey, the matter was referred to the Committee.'

A few Classes had already organised camps for their own members but here was a proposal which would bring together members from many places. So it was that eighteen months later, the first Union camp took place at Elmer, near Bognor Regis on the Sussex coast. It was a modest beginning comprising 13 officers and 31 boys, and no-one at the time could have foreseen what was to happen in the years ahead for, since then, thousands upon thousands of Crusaders have enjoyed wonderful holidays under the Crusaders' flag.

What was it that made, and still makes, Crusader camping so unique and so enjoyable an experience? Not easily answered in a few sentences but the basic ingredient was, and has always been, a group of officers dedicated to Christ and concerned to serve Him in serving the youngsters under their care. This has meant that long before the start of each Camp, Houseparty or Expedition, every facet of the project has been brought before God in prayer as all those involved have prepared to carry out their responsibilities. Every effort is made to plan and provide adequately for body, mind and spirit so that each day is filled with a well organised and smooth running programme involving activities such as games of all kinds, competitions, tide fights and excursions, not forgetting very carefully supervised bathing which always included our specially devised 'buddy' system whereby every boy kept an eye on another boy and vice versa all the time they were in the water.

The first Crusader Camp at Elmer, Bognor, in 1908

Bembridge Camp in 1910

Felixstowe in 1933; as the weather was so hot there was a headgear competition and everyone was supplied with a length of free muslin!

The first Sportsman's Houseparty at Monkton Combe School, near Bath

Hacker at a Westbrook Camp in the 50's

At Studland in 1961

Enjoying the beach at Dyffryn, North Wales, in 1969

Holidays in the 80's and 90's

Holiday brochures old and new

Several weeks before the commencement of the holiday programme, a day conference in London brings together the majority of officers involved, when helpful talks are given on various aspects of Crusader camping and time is provided for the respective teams to get to know each other, to pray together and to allocate duties.

In earlier days there was a somewhat militaristic flavour in the titles given to the staff officers. There was the Commandant, Adjutant, Padre, Quarter-master and Sub-Quatermaster which happily provided friendly and acceptable nicknames for use by the campers, namely 'Commy', 'Adjy', 'Quarters' and 'Subby' while Padre remained unchanged. In recent years, it was decided that it would be best to drop these titles, so instead we now have Leader, Organ-iser, Assistant Organiser and Caterer, which no longer provide the same facility for a friendly nickname but, of course, today everyone calls everyone by their Christian name, irrespective of age which, to my old fashioned mind, seems a pity. In addition the brief early morning bathing parade, and the semi-serious daily tent inspection involving a competition for tidiness, have also largely gone in this casual age which seems to resent any evidence of formal discipline.

We were sometimes fortunate in having influential contacts which made possible some unusual outings from camp. For example on one occasion our 'Commy' at a camp at Felixstowe was Squadron Leader (later Air Com-modore) P J Wiseman and he was able to arrange a visit to the nearby seaplane base where the RAF team was preparing to win outright the Schneider Trophy in the Supermarine S6B at the fabulous speed of 340.08 mph! We not only had the opportunity to view the seaplane at close quarters, we were also given a somewhat frightening demonstration as Squadron Leader Orlebar, one of the team, flew the machine low over our heads! Little did we guess we were seeing an early model of an aircraft which was ultimately to develop into the 'Spitfire' of World War II.

On another occasion at Studland Bay Camp, we discovered that the Adjutant - (a real one!) at the 'Armoured Fighting Vehicle and Gunnery School' at nearby Lulworth, was an old Finchley Crusader and he readily pro-vided us with an exciting demonstration, laid on specially for our benefit, which included the opportunity for all our campers to experience a ride - a very bumpy ride - in a tank.

In less sophisticated days, when folk were still used to making their own entertainment, the evening 'sing-song' was a must which provided enormous fun because in most camps considerable talent could often be found. Each camp had its platform and piano in the main marquee and the standard of performance was sometimes quite high. I still recall with pleasure, listening to a very young camper as he played piano solos and also accompanied our singing.   He was Herrick Bunney, who later became organist and choirmaster at St Giles Cathedral in Edinburgh.

Another gifted camper was Clifford Lucy, a Leader of the Stroud Green class; he accompanied his own songs on the piano in a thoroughly professional way. Incidentally he saw an advertisement one day in 'The Times' newspaper for a job vacancy which attracted him. It was typical of Clifford that instead of a formal application he applied for the job in verse!... and secured the appointment!! One of his many songs, composed at camp, remained a great favourite for many years, the chorus of which went something like this:

'Come to Cru camp,
Come to Cru camp,
That is the best place to be.
All who do camp
Say that Cru camp
Gives most for your £ s d.
The salt sea air
Blows everywhere,
Supplied entirely free.
With a mile or more
Of the choicest shore
And several pints of sea.'

Ludgate Hill had one of the first 'help yourself' restaurants in the City of London.   Clifford and I were lunching there about the time when Mr Chamberlain returned from Munich with Hitler's 'scrap of paper' promising peace. As we somewhat embarrassingly carried our trays to a vacant table (we were not used to tray carrying in those days!) Clifford said, "In spite of every-thing, I fear war with Germany is inevitable and many of us will not survive it." Words which sadly were tragically true for many Crusaders and also for him - he was killed in action. The other day I walked down Ludgate Hill, the place where that restaurant stood was still a deserted bomb site and wild flowers were growing where once we carried our trays, hoped for peace and prepared for camp.

In those earlier days no camp sing-song would be complete until the 'Editor' and his 'office boy' had read from their daily edition of the 'Camp Rag', a mock newspaper which consisted of humorous comment on camp life in general and camp officers in particular. Here is an extract from the 'Pwllheli Piffler' - Telegraphic Address - 'Razorblades Wrexham'.

'From our motoring correspondent. We have noticed quite a number of cars in camp and decided that Commy's car might make an interesting report - actually on touching the self-starter it made a simply enormous report! Perhaps this was to be expected for, after all, Commy is one of the Big Guns in camp. Incidentally, it has been said - 'the bigger the gun the bigger the bore'.

Commy's car has a one-and-a-half pint, 20 mouse-power Huntley and Palmer engine and is of revolutionary design, except for the wheels which don't take very readily to ideas of revolution.

On getting into the car, we noted it had a collapsible hood - unfortunately this state of collapse now appears to have become permanent.

We also noticed an unusual feature in that this vehicle has an emergency exit - through a big hole in the floor! Commy proudly pointed out an ultra modern invention of his own which enables the headlamps to be dimmed. All the driver has to do is stop the car, run round to the front and turn down the wick!

The horn made a colossal noise - at least we thought it was the horn and then suddenly realised that it was only Commy blowing his nose. I thought of the old Latin tag - 'Nostrom Commy snortibus'. I asked Commy how much he got out of his car, to which he immediately replied about 4 times per mile! Apparently he spends a lot of time going back to look for nuts - especially in May!

Commy then offered to demonstrate the speed of this breath-taking vehicle, and running into Pwllheli all down hill, we touched 20... and killed three more! There is just one feature in which this car is unique - the engine only requires to be run for five minutes and the water in the radiator is boiling and one can then have a hot bath or, if preferred, a cup of tea.'

Perhaps this little sample of camp humour may not seem particularly funny as you read it 'in cold blood'; but in the happy atmosphere and warm-hearted fellowship of a camping holiday, a hundred or more Crusaders would roar with laughter at yet another leg-pull at the expense of one of the staff. Those with camp experience will understand!

Yet another ingredient, also carefully planned and provided for, is perhaps the main reason why camps became so meaningful to so many. When Crusaders go to camp, they accept as perfectly natural, the holding of a Crusader type meeting, usually towards the end of each day. Most campers have been members of their respective classes for a considerable time during which the seed of God's Word has been sown regularly in their hearts and minds. The atmosphere at camp provides an ideal setting for some of that seed to come to fruition as the challenge of Christ's call to faith and discipleship is presented as a choice to be made. During my time with Crusaders I have met literally hundreds of boys, young and not so young men, who happily and gratefully refer to camp as the place where a wholehearted trust in Christ as Saviour and Lord became really meaningful and so had altered the whole course of their lives. More often than not many of these same boys graduated in due time to become camp officers themselves, rejoicing at the opportunity to help the youngsters in their tent – or dormitory if it was a houseparty – to find Christ, the Saviour, Friend and Lord, they themselves had come to know in earlier days while enjoying the best of all holidays.

As I write I have before me the Crusader Holidays brochure for the coming year listing more than fifty Camps, Houseparties and Ventures. There are Holidays with special interests: canoeing, cycling, football, pony trekking, rail enthusiasts, sailing, skiing, sports and watersports ... and several Work Parties where the aim is to be useful by serving the community in various ways such as working with mentally handicapped children at the Cheyne Centre in Kent or spending time with young patients at the Royal National Orthopaedic Hospital. Another party will be helping at the Mayflower Family Centre in East London, while others will be making themselves available to serve the National Trust in Cumbria by digging ditches, repairing footpaths and similar duties. All the members of these Work Parties pay normal fees – it's not a question of 'Working your Passage'!

So the 44 pioneers in 1908 started something which now involves hundreds of young people, nor is this the whole story for many of the larger Classes or groups of Classes, organise their own camps and houseparties, both at Easter and during the summer months. It would be hard to exaggerate the value of the part played by all these Crusader activities for not only do the young people meet each other in a happy, well organised and healthy environment but, for many it has consequences the extent of which is known only to God, but we do know enough to give cause for heartfelt praise because He has so continuously crowned the camps, houseparties and expeditions with so much lasting blessing.

7

GROWING PAINS

The years immediately following the founding of the Union saw steady growth and much encouragement; by the Spring of 1914 there were 43 Classes with more than 70 Leaders and a total membership of more than 3,000 boys. However the very growth of the Union was causing problems because it meant the burden of administration was also increasing. Many of the Leaders, particularly those in the London area, were involved in Committee and Sub-Committee work in addition to running their own Classes; most were also office bearers in the churches to which they belonged.

Then there was the planning and staffing of the Summer Camps which in 1909, 1910 and 1911 were held at Whitecliff Bay in Bembridge on the Isle of Wight, with a move to Ladram Bay, Devon in 1913. In 1911 Mr Tom Priestman, who was Leader of the Hull Class, decided to organise a camp for the benefit of the Classes which had been formed in the Northern part of England and this took place at Hunmanby Gap, near Filey in Yorkshire. It was a great success and proved to be the first of many which, in subsequent years, were held in that part of the country.

Leaders' Conferences were held annually and every other year there were Rallies in London which, by 1914, brought together 1,300 Crusaders to the City of London School near Blackfriars Bridge. In connection with this the records relate:

'The Rev A C Kestin presided, and introduced Mr Frank Wild FRGS, who came to lecture on Antarctic Exploration, in the place of Sir Ernest Shackleton. The lecture was illustrated with Lantern Slides and held the audience spell-bound as the lecturer related his adventures amidst the snow and ice, mountains and glaciers of the South Polar Region.'

All this activity and growth convinced the General Committee that the time had come to appoint a paid Secretary who could give all his time to the movement and, quoting again from the records, we learn that:

'The appointment of Mr H J Clark to the secretaryship has been amply justified by the record of 1913. Leaders have been able to give time individually to their Classes, leaving the secretarial work to be centralised and carried through by Mr Clark. This has had the effect of relief all round, and has liberated energies in other directions.'

One of those 'other directions' was the devising of a Constitution which would enshrine officially in writing the aims and objects of the movement, the appointing of various officers and the method of their appointment, also the general structure and administration of the work.

At that time there were influential theologians, involved in what was termed 'Higher Criticism', who were questioning the veracity of Scripture, so it is not surprising to find in the Constitution the following paragraph, to which reference has already been made:

'The whole of the Bible shall be taught at the Bible Classes as the Word of God, and a thorough Evangelical and Protestant spirit maintained, the Classes remaining interdenominational and working as far as possible in harmony with the local churches.'

These words were to act as a sheet anchor in the ensuing years as the spread of the so called 'liberal theology' undermined the confidence of so many ministers and lay people in the trustworthiness of the Bible, the result of which was the blunting of any evangelical thrust in many churches and Christian movements, so their respective trumpets gave an uncertain sound with the inevitable result that increasingly few prepared themselves for the battle.

Today the term 'Higher Criticism' has been forgotten because much of what those earlier theologians so confidently asserted has been disproved by modern scholarship but, sadly, the seeds of doubt they sowed with such assurance has resulted in a harvest of unbelief and so today in all too many pul-

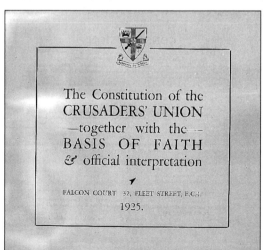

pits 'Thus saith the Lord', or its equivalent, is conspicuous by its absence. It takes a Billy Graham to assert repeatedly 'The Bible says'!

The Constitution of the
CRUSADERS' UNION
—together with the —
BASIS OF FAITH
& official interpretation

FALCON COURT 32, FLEET STREET, E.C.4.
1925.

8

RUMOURS OF WAR

Alas, it wasn't just a rumour for on 4th August 1914 the German army, on the order of Kaiser Wilhelm, began the invasion of Belgium and soon Belgian refugees were arriving in Britain. War, of course, was the responsibility of the Army and Navy, or had been until now; this time however it was different, volunteers were called for and men everywhere responded to Kitchener's challenging poster from which he seemed to be looking and pointing directly at the onlooker with the accompanying words: 'YOUR COUNTRY NEEDS YOU'. Soon patriotic songs were being sung – 'It's a long way to Tipperary' and 'Keep the home fires burning'.

In the preface to the Union Report for 1914, reference is made to the effect of the war as follows:

'Until the end of the Summer term of 1914, great progress on all hands was noted. In a movement such as the 'Crusaders' comprising so large a number of potential soldiers, the effect of the sudden call to arms was immediate and immense. Distasteful and repugnant as war must generally be to the Christian mind, here was a call so resistless and urgent that a number of leaders and a great proportion of our senior membership at once responded.'

In fact more than a thousand Crusaders had already joined up of whom more than twenty had been killed – it was only the beginning.

It had been intended to hold three Camps in the Summer holidays of 1914, at Sandsend near Whitby, Pagham near Bognor and Saunton in Devon. The one at Sandsend was carried through despite difficulties but the others had to be cancelled. Twenty-five years later history was to repeat itself.

It was a severe testing time for all concerned. Mr H J Clark, the recently appointed Secretary, left to join the Army in October 1914 and so once again the secretarial work had to be done by the remaining Leaders and Mr H B Stevenson, Leader of Upper Tooting Class, assumed the duties of Honorary Secretary.

Now it was a case of finding older men willing to try and maintain Classes which had become leaderless, often at very short notice. I recall how the Muswell Hill Class, which I later joined, was cared for by two gentlemen unfit

Hendon Crusaders – 1915

for war service, one was blind and the other crippled by polio – but the work
went on.

At first it was predicted that the war would be over in a few weeks, but
month after month went by until in the Union Report for the year 1915/16
we read that:

'The sternness and urgency of the demands made by the War have been felt
in an ever-increasing degree, so that in May 1916, we find that there are few
Classes that have not lost one or more of its leaders, and every Class has given
its senior members. By the end of the summer term, the position will be a
precarious one, and it appears likely that some Classes must close till better
days come again.'

The writer's words proved all too accurate, it was a sad time for many, few
families escaped receiving the dreaded telegram bringing the tragic news of
father or son 'killed in action'. The slaughter was devastating and it went on
and on.

For the first time in its history civilian Britain suffered air raids. The aircraft
of those days were slow moving by today's standards and I recall how we

received advance warning of impending raids from Wardens on bicycles touring the roads calling out 'Take Cover' and repeating the process later with the cry of 'All Clear'! Bombs were not only delivered by aeroplanes but by Zeppelins also, which were large airships named after Count F Von Zeppelin their inventor and constructor. They appeared a frightening menace as our powerful searchlights easily picked them out in the darkness; what is more they seemed impervious to gun fire as they sailed majestically by, bullets apparently went through the envelope doing very little damage, until one night I recall vividly how the members of my family, as we sheltered behind the upturned dining room table, suddenly rose up and ran outside for we could hear our neighbours apparently cheering with delight – as indeed they were. A few miles to the north of us, a Zeppelin, held in the rays of searchlights was seen to be on fire. At first, flames could be seen licking around the whale-like shape, then it broke in the centre, folded and began to descend as a ball of flame.

It transpired that an incendiary bullet had just been invented and this was the first occasion it had been used on Zeppelins. The memory of that night will remain for ever in my mind, the more so as I sometimes pass the monument in Cuffley, Herts, which commemorates the occasion and the place where the Zeppelin came down, also the German crew that perished with it.

And so the War dragged on, but turning over the papers of the Annual Report for 1916 we come upon a paragraph of considerable significance; here it is:

'A Union of Girls' Classes was formed last year, with the object of bringing existing Girls' Classes together, in the same way as was done with boys' Classes in the early days of our Union. In the hope that the publicity given may be of service in extending the work, we give below particulars of the present Classes. The Secretary is Miss Bacon, 30 Rosemount Road, Acton, who will gladly answer any enquiries. For this work also we ask the remembrance of friends, as the opportunities of extension are here also very great.'

Then follows a list of twenty-two Classes together with the names and addresses of their Leaders. True to the accepted attitudes of those days, the two movements were regarded as completely separate in every respect. After all 'girls were girls and boys were boys' and even in the local situation there was virtually no contact whatsoever, which today will seem odd but then was perfectly normal and acceptable.

Some years later there was a slight change when a few areas formed mixed fellowships which met monthly, or occasionally, on a weeknight evening, and catered for senior boys and girls in neighbouring Classes; but I recall that for the most part there was very little mixing even then.

And so the War dragged on and reports from the various Classes reveal how badly the Union was being hit. For example the Finchley Class:

'Like many another Class, our attendance is not what it used to be in pre-war days. We are very proud of 170 past and present members we have given to fight in the cause of freedom, but this has, of course, meant a considerable drain on our resources, which it is difficult to make good in these times of high-pressure work, when visiting is out of the question. Sunday 23rd June was a red-letter day for us when we had the pleasure of once again seeing our old Leaders, Mr H Bevington and Mr H V Lidington, who were both on leave. Mr Bevington, whom we had not seen for eleven months, gave us a very interesting talk about his work (RNAS motor-boats) and the impression it made on him.'

I cannot refrain from including this brief extract from the Crusaders' Magazine about a Leader whose life, teaching and living example has meant so much to me and many others:

'Our dear friend and old Leader of the Muswell Hill Class, Lieut Jack Freegard, has lost all his kit and belongings in the Big Push, but has himself escaped unhurt, for which we all rejoice. May God still preserve him.'

Perhaps the tensions, trials and challenge of those war years can best be conveyed by a letter which was printed in the Magazine, it read as follows:

'My Dear Fellow Crusaders. I have been asked to write a few lines from France to pass on any thoughts or tips that might be of help to you who are coming out shortly for the first time. As Crusaders we have nothing to fear if our faith is real and so long as we keep a consciousness of His presence ever near us, all will be well. During fourteen months of continuous line work, in the attack, in raids or just holding the line, it has been my joy and privilege to experience the perfect peace that passeth man's under-standing.

Let me pass on the last words my chum, Leslie Elvey (Streatham Crusaders) spoke to me before I said goodbye to him for the last time on earth just as I left to go up the line. The train was just leaving a certain station on the Belgian border, travelling towards the Ypres salient, and dear old Elvey called after me, "Goodbye, don't forget Isaiah 26:3, 'Thou wilt keep him in perfect peace whose mind is stayed on Thee'." Just twenty-four hours from that parting I was receiving my baptism of fire. I was in the line for the very first time and hadn't been in the frontline trenches more than half-an-hour before the Huns raided. These words flashed through my mind; I felt His presence even in that deafening barrage and experienced perfect peace. From that moment to this I have never known His peace fail through the most terrible experiences.... God be with you all and bless you, is the earnest prayer of a Croydon Crusader, Howard J Rose (Capt).'

9

FORWARD MARCH

It came at long last - at the eleventh hour, of the eleventh day, of the eleventh month in 1918, the Armistice was signed and the War was over - but at what a cost! Approximately three thousand Crusaders had joined the armed forces during those years of strife, of which some three hundred were never to return home. 'The flower of young manhood whose loss we deeply deplore and whose memory we desire to cherish' are words taken from the report of a memorial service for the Crusaders who had been killed; it was held in London on 25th April 1919 in St Andrew's Church, Holborn.

The experiences of war tend to clarify values and many Crusaders on returning to 'Civvy Street' were eager to devote their spare time to Christian work and, where appropriate, to the Union. Not least among them was one Amos John Vereker who, when a boy at Highgate School, had been a member of the Finchley Class and was now a Leader of the Hampstead Class meeting in University College School.

He had served as a Captain in the Machine Gun Corps during the War, where life expectation in the front line was four days! He had returned to England badly wounded and had been awarded the Military Cross. Now recovered, he was working in a Stockbroker's office, which his vigorous spirit found most frustrating, he longed to spend his life more directly working for the Kingdom of God.

About this time the General Committee were once again feeling the need for a full-time Secretary and the Minutes of their meeting on 23rd September 1919, held in the office of the Union, 36 Camomile Street, EC3, contain the following:

'Future Secretarial Arrangements. A suggestion was brought forward that Mr A J Vereker should be appointed as acting secretary for six months: such appointment being open to revision on both sides at any time during that period.'

The Minute goes on to appoint a Sub-Committee 'to interview Mr Vereker and to ascertain his views on such subjects as the inspiration of the Scriptures etc; the Sub-Committee were given power, if they considered Mr

Vereker satisfactory, to appoint him forthwith as secretary – 'pro tempore' for three months at a remuneration of £50'. The Minutes of the next meeting of the General Committee a month later, are recorded in the handwriting which became so familiar to me in the years that followed and tell how the members 'accorded him a warm welcome in his new duties'.

The October number of 'The Crusaders' Magazine' contains the following paragraph under the heading 'The Editor Thinks Aloud' (the Editor was the Rev Guy H King).

'The time has come for advance. During years of war we have had, perforce, to mark time, but now the word of command is 'Forward!'... The General Committee of the Union is prayerfully watchful for the right man to be our Secretary, and by the time this Magazine appears it is quite likely that a man will have been appointed.'

It was a very significant appointment and in the years that followed it became abundantly clear that once again 'The steps of a good man are ordered by the Lord'. Mr Vereker's warm hearted zeal was infectious, he never took 'No' for an answer as he travelled about on his motor cycle, persuading suitable men to open new Classes. Greatly loved by the officers and boys at Camp, he was always the Adjutant and soon became affectionately known as 'Adjy' throughout the Union. A natural actor, I've seen tears in campers' eyes as he sang a typical Victorian sentimental song entitled 'Jammy Face'.

From his father's side there was Irish blood in his veins which may have accounted in part for his attractive personality, but perhaps it also accounted for the strength with which he held particular doctrinal views, and also for taking daring action others would have hesitated even to consider.

For example I recall vividly the very first occasion on which we planned to hold a Rally in the Royal Albert Hall in 1932. There were those on the Committee who were extremely doubtful of the wisdom of such a venture. We could certainly fill the Central Hall, Westminster with its 2,500 seats but the Albert Hall with 7,000 or so – surely not! Mr Vereker had no such doubts, "Of course we'll fill it!"

Imagine his consternation when on receiving confirmation of the booking from the Albert Hall authorities, he learnt that many of the boxes and seats were actually owned privately, and all the owners had to be written to with a request to allow their tickets to be released on this particular occasion. It soon became evident that the owners who, of course, were always receiving such requests from hirers of the Hall, were fed up with having to reply and so many didn't bother; no doubt others were away from home. It looked as though the Hall would be half empty, but Mr Vereker had other ideas. Contrary to all the

A J Vereker, General Secretary 1919-1946
and first Warden of Westbrook

rules he arranged for several thousand tickets of admission to be printed without informing the Albert Hall authorities of his intention, and these extra tickets were sent to the Classes that wanted to attend the Rally, once all the available official tickets had been allocated.

At last the great day arrived, a day none of the Hall's official stewards will ever have forgotten! Thousands upon thousands of excited Crusaders poured into the Albert Hall and, when it was full to overflowing, kept on coming - and they all had tickets of admission! In the end the doors were shut and the stewards devised a scheme for coping with those milling around inside the building but with no seats available. They gave the impression that there were seats in another part of the Hall: 'down these stairs please follow me' but the stairs led only to exits and soon thousands of youngsters with their Leaders were outside, and now locked out!

As Gilbert and Sullivan proclaimed in another context, it was 'a pretty how-d'you-do', those outside were very distressed and annoyed and justifiably so; Leaders had brought their members from all over the country and now this! Their feelings of frustration and disappointment were intense. In the end an impromptu open-air gathering was held on the steps of the Albert memorial opposite and some of the speakers taking part inside the Hall, came outside and addressed the assembly - but it was all very unfortunate.

Those inside the Hall had a wonderful time, never before had so many Crusaders come together in one place and it was an inspiration to everyone there. Of course every seat was taken and so was every nook and cranny; I'm certain the Hall had never before accommodated so many, and I'm sure it hasn't done so since. Mr Vereker undoubtedly holds the record!

I leave you to imagine the sequel and also the size of our postbag in the days that followed, but our worthy Secretary was not greatly upset, he had achieved his object of filling the Albert Hall and, having dodged most of the German bullets in the War, he was not afraid of the verbal brickbats that came his way. Of course he apologised profusely and was soon forgiven – but only a person with a measure of Irish blood....!!

It will be remembered that Mr Vereker's appointment was 'pro tempore' but it quickly became abundantly clear to the Committee that here was the man for the job, and his appointment was confirmed on 1st March 1920 – a position he was to hold for more than a quarter of a century.

During most of the War years, as already mentioned, the position of Honorary Acting Secretary had been held by Mr Harold B Stevenson, a Leader of the Upper Tooting Class. He was a chartered accountant and had used his office as a temporary Union Headquarters. Now that a full-time Secretary had been appointed it was necessary to seek some other HQ location and, once again, the CSSM provided welcome help. Their Secretary, Mr J H Hubbard, who was also a member of the Crusader Union's General Committee, offered a small room in his offices at 13a Warwick Lane, a road off Ludgate Hill. Minutes of the Committee meeting on 6th April 1920 record that: 'the Union was greatly indebted to the CSSM for their kindness in the matter'. Under the heading 'cheques signed' on that day is one for £3 17s 0d for 'Office furniture'; Mr Vereker was beginning to establish a Union Headquarters!

At that same meeting a decision was taken which, at the time, must have seemed somewhat trivial, but one, the value of which it would be hard to exaggerate. Here it is:

'Mr Bevington on behalf of the Sub-Committee which was appointed to enquire into a proposal for the formation of an Associate Membership Branch, presented a draft form of application for membership, which was accepted after a few alterations had been made.'

The intention was to enable senior Crusaders to keep in touch with the Union when the time came for them to leave their Classes, which was usually to participate in Sunday School or some other Christian activity. Since that time thousands upon thousands of Crusaders have retained their link with the

Union in this way, and their interest and their prayer support have been sustained by receiving Magazines and other informative literature regularly. It could scarcely be possible to over-estimate what this has meant to the spiritual health and vitality of Crusaders, and without their generous and continuing financial support the movement could never have developed in the way it has done.

As I pen these words my mind goes to the story of the building, or rather the re-building of the Temple in Jerusalem when the word of the Lord came to Zechariah saying: "Who hath despised the day of small things?" (Zech 4.10) a question which certainly seems appropriate here.

During those early post-war years the growth of the Union was steady rather than spectacular: on average one new Class was elected every other month and by 1922 numbers had risen to approximately 4,500 members in 58 Classes. However it was not long before Mr Vereker felt the need for some help in the office and a Miss Hobson was employed for four hours per day, soon to be replaced by a Miss Casswell, a shorthand typist who continued to work at Headquarters until 1929.

At the meeting of the General Committee in April 1922 Mr J H Hubbard, regretfully stated 'that he may be forced to request the Union Committee to seek an office elsewhere in the autumn. He assured the Committee that he would do everything in his power to delay this move – which must come shortly on account of the growth of the Union.'

Happily enough an answer to the need was speedily forthcoming for at the meeting of the General Committee two months later: 'It was reported that the Church of England Scripture Readers' Association would be willing to receive an offer for the use of their offices'. This would provide an 'inner room' for the Secretary and the share of a larger outer office, in company with the Society's clerk. The Committee's offer of £60 per annum was accepted. It was actually a sub-let for the building was owned by, and was the Headquarters of the Church Pastoral Aid Society. The move took place on Tuesday, 18th July 1922 and the Union's new address was Falcon Court, 32 Fleet Street, EC4.

An interesting commentary on attitudes is provided in a General Committee Minute at this time; it refers to a letter having been received from Mrs Bacon, who had taken over from Miss Bacon as the Hon Secretary of the Girl Crusaders' Union, suggesting the holding of a joint annual meeting for Crusaders and Girl Crusaders. Evidently the idea was not at all welcome for:

'It was decided to inform Mrs Bacon that while the General Committee would be most happy to invite the girls to our meeting, and if desired reserve

for them the Balcony of the hall, it was felt that to arrange any kind of com-
bined meeting would be unwise. It was suggested that the Girl Crusaders
might arrange to hold their Annual Meeting in the Autumn.'

How times have changed!

10

OUR OWN HEADQUARTERS

As already mentioned, the Minutes of the monthly Committee meetings in those days always contained a record of cheques signed and of the balance which would be left in credit at the bank. For most of the time this would only amount to a few pounds and, not infrequently, some cheques had to be held back for a week or two in order to avoid going into the red. In fact all through the years we at Headquarters were exceedingly careful with our spending, anxious that it would never become a burden or an embarrassment to the leadership or to the Union as a whole. The Leaders and their Classes must always come first; Headquarters was there to serve and to support them - not the other way round.

Of course in those days, no office could be regarded as fully operational without an 'Office boy', although by now he may have become an extinct species or is perhaps called by a more high sounding name in the way in which old fashioned 'dustmen' have been replaced by 'refuse collectors'!

Be that as it may a brief minute records the fact that Mr Vereker was given permission to appoint an office boy at a wage of ten shillings (50p) per week, and there came to work at HQ a young member of the Cambridge University Mission in Bermondsey, named Solomon Adamsbaum. As you may have guessed he was not a Gentile and even had you not known his name, his throaty voice and distinctive looks proclaimed his Jewish ancestry - but he was an 'out and out' Christian and a most lovable and warm-hearted character. He served the Union devotedly for several years before leaving to join the staff of one of the Christian Missions to Jews. It would be hard to imagine anyone more suited to that specialised work.

It is true to say that the Union has been most fortunate in its choice of office boys for, in due course, 'Solly', as he was affectionately known, was promoted to more important work in the office, so that in 1926 a successor was required. A young member of the Boys' Brigade was appointed named Daniel J Mahony. Little did he, or anyone else for that matter, guess that fifty years later he would still be serving the Union at Headquarters! A wonderful record of faithful, devoted and self-giving service.

In recalling those early days he particularly remembers dreading Thursdays; there had been appointed a General Purposes Sub-Committee which met at lunchtime each Thursday to deal with Union business – about which more later. Dan Mahony had to cross over busy Fleet Street to a Jo Lyons tea-shop opposite, and fetch hot roast beef and two veg, together with apple pie, in sufficient quantity to satisfy the appetites of some half-dozen members who ate as they discussed Union affairs. In a recent letter he told me, 'The feeling of awe and dread I experienced serving the revered gentlemen, I still remember well!'.

His letter continues: 'Mr Vereker would take Wednesday afternoons off to play golf with his friend and flatmate E P Olney (who for many years was Leader of the Putney Class). Solly and I used to play football in his room until one day we broke the window and retribution followed!' No doubt they had forgotten what Paul said to Timothy, 'bodily exercise profiteth little!'. Perhaps that is why in Dan's early days at HQ Mr Vereker insisted on giving him a daily dose of cod liver oil. I can't help feeling there must be a moral somewhere in all this! One thing is certain, as he developed in physique he also developed a delightful Christian character: he and I were together at HQ for forty years with never once a cross or unkindly word between us. Gentle in manner, always reliable, he was faithfulness personified; his stable influence on our staff was invaluable. Over the years we employed dozens of young men and girls and they invariably poured out all their youthful problems in Dan's understanding ears and went on their way comforted and assured.

The Summer of 1928 saw two significant developments both of which are recorded in the minutes of the General Committee in the following way:

'Financial Position. The Secretary stated that he had received cheques, or promises for, in all £120 towards the Forward Movement, from Leaders. He also stated he believed within two years the profit on books etc, in the new offices would more than pay for the increased rent: another £160 per annum would be required in connection with the appointment of an Accountant.'

The time had come to acquire a Headquarters sufficiently large to provide facilities for a bookroom, and there was a need for an accountant, not only to deal with money received and bills paid, but also to supervise the purchase and sale of stock for a bookroom, and to handle applications for Camps, Easter Houseparties, and Conferences, items which were taking up too much of the Secretary's time.

The new offices were on the first floor of No 4, New Bridge Street, overlooking Ludgate Circus, and the accountant was to be Stephen Cox who had been a leader of Glasgow South Class, and was shortly to transfer his leadership to Wandsworth Common Class.

Dan Mahony – 50 years' faithful service at Headquarters

Once the staff had settled in, Leaders were invited to a reception in the new offices - 'and were served with tea'. Like most City offices of those days, the new Headquarters was far from palatial; approached by narrow winding stairs, the front door opened on to a large room, and leading from it down a few steps was another room considerably smaller but sufficiently large to accommodate the General Committee meetings and also to serve as the Secretary's room.

Solly, Dan and the typist occupied part of the large room, the other part was to see the gradual establishment of a bookroom but it was quite some time before a bookcase was constructed which also provided a partial division and made one section look more like a real bookroom. There was no bookroom staff as such, but Solly or Dan would be available when service was needed. Stephen Cox had a small 'cubby hole' in one corner of the room, created by a temporary partition which gave a semblance of privacy and provided only just enough room for a desk, a chair and a safe. It was very cramped and I write feelingly for I sat at that same desk for nine years until the outbreak of World War II. The Union was continuing to grow at an encouraging rate but the Headquarters always subsisted on a 'shoestring', every penny had to be watched, after all we were a missionary society and like all good missionary societies, resources must be devoted mainly to work 'in the field'. For example, in January 1931, Stephen Cox approached the Chairman and informed him of his wish to get married. The Committee discussed the proposition at their February meeting when: 'It was unanimously decided that no increase in salary could be made at the moment, but that the position would be reviewed later in the year although no promise of advancement could be made.'

It was not an unreasonable decision for those days, however Stephen decided to seek pastures new and he joined the staff of the British and Foreign Bible Society where his first appointment was to Bangalore in South India.

No doubt the Committee's deliberations were affected, at least in part, by a very significant appointment made at that same meeting. For several years, a Leader of the St Albans Class had found much acceptance as a visiting speaker at neighbouring Classes and, as time went on, he began to conduct special evangelistic weekends which would include a Saturday Squash, with a talk, and an additional meeting after Class and tea on the Sunday. Invariably there was blessing and boys were converted. His name was Laurence C Head and because he seemed to overflow with loving concern when speaking, he earned the nickname of 'Bubbly', it could not have been more apt!

In 1931 he had reached the stage in his life when, as the Minute records: 'Mr Head was seeking either whole-time work in the Lord's service, or a new partnership in business'. Those who knew him well might perhaps have smiled at the idea of Laurence Head as a 'business man' but when it came to his gift as an evangelist among boys, he was second to none. Not that he had the slick repartee of many a professional evangelist with a fund of stories; but somehow his simple, genuine, uncomplicated boyishness won the hearts and minds of youngsters in a quite remarkable way, it was so obviously a gift from God. He rarely called for any outward display of conversion, instead he asked those concerned to accept a leaflet of his own entitled: 'Steps to Christ and Steps with Christ' and invited boys to write and tell him if they had been helped. Most boys hate writing letters but 'Bubbly' was not looking for emotional decisions but Spirit motivated conversions which would be genuine – and the letters would arrive – sometimes many letters and the boys' Leaders would be informed so that each 'new born babe' could be fed and cared for and prayerfully supported. Over the years that followed I sometimes wondered how many boys had been converted through his simple ministry, but he wasn't interested in numbers, he was happy in the knowledge that he was part

Laurence Head – lovingly known as 'Bubbly'

of a team of Leaders who, over the years, had planted the precious seed of the Word and had faithfully watered it with their prayers, and now God had given the increase in accordance with 1 Corinthians 3:6. I can't help exclaiming 'Dear old Bubbly' - he couldn't even add up his expense list correctly which he brought to me from time to time to settle, it was hard enough to decipher let alone to check!

In later years he frequently organised Easter Houseparties and I was often amazed when I heard him introduce himself over the phone to a Headmaster whose school he wanted to hire - it went like this: "This is Laurence Head speaking... Travelling Secretary of the Crusaders' Union whose President is the Lord Chief Justice of England!" It was all true of course - but I couldn't help wondering what sort of a picture was created in the mind of the Head-master as he listened - a knight in shining armour perhaps and undoubtedly on horseback with sword raised in salute! - but he often got the school!

So it was that at that February meeting in 1931, it was unanimously decided to invite Mr Head to join the HQ staff for one year, his duties to be:

★ To co-operate with the Secretary in the extension of the work of the Union.

★ To visit Classes as invited and conduct weekend Campaigns.

★ To advise and help Leaders as required.

★ To attend Camps and weekend Houseparties and Conferences.

So began an association which lasted almost forty years although it soon became clear there was not a lot he could do during the week and, in due course, he was appointed Secretary of the Christian Colportage Association but continued as the Union's Travelling Secretary at weekends and was available for Camps and Houseparties: a gift of God indeed.

11

BASIS OF BELIEF

As mentioned earlier, soon after the founding of the Union in 1906, a Constitution was introduced, which laid down the aims and objects of the movement, it also dealt with the method of the election of officers, the duties of the Committee and in fact all matters necessary to ensure a business-like administration. As the work developed so alterations and amendments were made and in 1921 it was felt advisable to include in the Constitution a 'Basis of Belief' because, as also referred to previously, certain doctrines which until then had been taken for granted, were now being questioned by so-called expert theologians.

At the Annual Business Meeting in April 1921 the proposed basis was presented to the leadership for consideration, by the Chairman of the Sub-Committee appointed to examine the matter. His name, R R Webster, will bring back happy memories to some older readers. He said that the members of the Sub-Committee had felt that six short clauses would be sufficient to safeguard the Union's position. They had done their work well for the proposed wording was adopted there and then, and has remained unchanged ever since. And so the Basis which every Class Leader is required to accept before being elected by the General Committee is as follows:

(1) *God as the Creator of all men, and the Father of all who believe in the Lord Jesus Christ.*

(2) *The Lord Jesus Christ as the only begotten Son of God, Redeemer of the World, and the one Mediator, through faith in whom alone we obtain forgiveness of sins.*

(3) *God the Holy Spirit.*

(4) *The fact of sin, and the necessity for the Atonement.*

(5) *The Incarnation, Death, Resurrection, Ascension and Coming Again of the Lord Jesus Christ.*

(6) *The whole Bible as the Inspired Word of God.*

The Committee's decision to have a Basis of Belief was a wise one for since that time there has been onslaught after onslaught on basic Christian doctrines and the Basis has ensured that those attracted to the possibility of Crusader leadership recognised the condition under which, among other things, their applications would be considered.

Perhaps we should not be surprised that every now and again there arises a situation or a deviation which can seem attractive to some Christians and even to some Crusader Leaders. Older readers will recall the arrival of Dr Buchman from America and the introduction of so-called 'Buchmanism' with its doctrine of absolutes, its emphasis on the 'Quiet Time' and the requirement that sins be confessed to one another.

Of course the encouragement to give more time to waiting upon God brought personal blessing, but certain other facets were questionable. I recall the Committee producing a leaflet which advised Leaders to steer clear. Incidentally Buchmanism later became known as the 'Oxford Group Movement'.

I remember with sadness an occasion, in a quite different context, when a much-loved Leader who had done a lot in earlier days to help establish the Union, became attracted to a translation of the Bible called the 'Concordant Version', again from America! If memory serves me aright, the belief behind this production was the idea that when translating the Scriptures each Greek word could only have one English equivalent irrespective of context.

The Committee members felt sure the translation was spurious and were so advised by Christian scholars, but the Leader in question remained unmoved and taught his Class from its pages. At last in a final attempt to persuade him of his unwisdom, the Committee engaged the services of a Professor of Greek at London University with the request that he should examine the version in question and record his views on its soundness as a translation. He was not informed of the reason for the assignment.

His report tore to shreds the translation and the reasoning behind it, and with great relief the Committee presented the Leader with the Professor's unbiased findings, certain that reason would now prevail. Alas it made no difference and, after much heart searching, members felt obliged to terminate his leadership because he refused to resign. It was a deeply hurtful experience to all concerned for such a thing had never happened before - nor has it since.

But there were other attacks from time to time. Satan is always active where worthwhile work is being done in the name of Christ, and one of his tricks, if he can't hold Christians back, is to trade on their very zeal and push them on to foolish extravagancies. So it was that a group of tremendously zealous young Crusaders, deeply concerned to be the best for God and at any price, decided to give up their jobs and went off to a certain Bible College in

Wales. They had been persuaded that unless they were willing to give God all their time and possessions, they were not fully committed disciples, and didn't Luke 14:33 confirm their action?

I recall Mr Vereker's anger at the person, who had no connection with the Union, whose persuasiveness had brought this about; and off he went to Wales to beard the lion in his den. Eventually those involved returned home sadder and wiser from their experience, and no doubt a good deal poorer too. As I write the faces and names of one or two other much loved Leaders come to mind, from down the years, whose zeal was greater than their wisdom and who, as a result suffered nervous breakdowns and, for a time, a complete loss of faith. Ecclesiastes 7:16 is not a verse often quoted or even noticed but is very relevant to any in danger of losing their balance spiritually. 'Be not righteous overmuch; neither make thyself overwise: why shouldest thou destroy thyself?'

Satan is always up to something, I sometimes wonder what are his modern strategies? If I were allowed to speculate I would question the introduction of gimmicks into some very worthy communities which, to me, seem to savour of religious entertainment rather than worship in spirit and in truth.

Another question in my mind relates to many of the songs popular in Christian circles today, which appear so poor in content compared with the songs of the past which we called choruses. The majority of those choruses were objective and Scriptural, looking away from self to the wonder of God's love and provision in Christ, with the promise of power to keep the believer faithful. Today many of the songs I hear appear subjective and centred on *me* worshipping God or *me* doing His will, and sometimes linked with a pithy bit of Scripture that seems almost irrelevant, eg 'My tongue is the pen of a ready writer'.

No doubt I'm out of date and biased, and it's so easy to criticise but I can't help feeling a deep-down concern at what appears to be an increase in religious emotion and a decrease in spirituality based on solid Scriptural foundations.

Turi Crusaders in Kenya in the 80's

12

CLASSES ABROAD

It will be clear from what has been related so far, that the Union had been started to meet a particular need in England, a need which had become more evident with the passing years. The possibility of the movement extending its boundaries had never been seriously considered for, generally speaking the majority of our Welsh, Scottish and Irish neighbours still comprised quite close-knit church going communities and children were catered for in their respective Sunday Schools. So it came as quite a surprise when, out of the blue, a letter arrived from a Mr R C Findlay asking that his Bible Class in Melbourne, Australia be received into the Union. However after appropriate enquiries had been made, the Class was duly elected in July 1922, and in the years that followed, two further Classes came into being in Melbourne and Mr Findlay's fellow Leaders made him the 'Honorary Secretary for the Crusader Movement in Australia'. The Committee in London decided to recognise Mr Findlay's appointment; supplied him with literature and badges and agreed to accept his local Committee's appointments to leadership which would be subject to confirmation. In 1928 when there were still only three Classes, the Committee 'decided to recognise in some way or other the work of Mr Findlay' and their token of appreciation took the form of a Scofield Reference Bible, which in those days was highly regarded.

As time went by the Committee began to feel that the arrangement with Australia was not very satisfactory mainly because communication was so slow. A letter to Mr Findlay had to go by sea, and it would be received four, five or sometimes six weeks after despatch. The reply would take a similar time and so there would be an interval of two months, at the very least, between a letter and its reply. Understandably the Committee felt concern at having responsibility for work in a country so far away and in circumstances with which they could not be familiar. Reluctantly they came to the conclusion to 'close down the work in Australia' much to the disappointment of the Leaders there. However this did not mean an end to the movement which, under the Crusader name developed and prospered for many years, but Sunday classes were gradually replaced by meetings in schools each one of which was called a 'Crusader Union' rather like a Christian Union in a British school, but in their case normally led by adults. In due course Scripture Union took the place of Crusaders and a fine work continues to this day. There are still some Crusader Union groups in New South Wales.

During this time 'Crusaders' also came into being in New Zealand and here too it seemed sensible for them to develop independently in association with Scripture Union. As I write I have before me Volume 1, Number 2 of their quarterly magazine entitled 'Standfast', published in December 1950; it begins with an editorial by Professor E M Blaiklock. Incidentally it was in New Zealand that Dr John Laird became fully involved in the CSSM and Scripture Union work. I notice with interest that this number of their magazine contains an article from a Mary Milner, an ex-Crusader working with the China Inland Mission on the borders of Tibet. Mary had been a member of the group at Welling East Girls' College and, before going to China, had served the Crusader Movement for ten years and had been Dr Laird's first secretary.

As many readers will recall, in due course Dr Laird came back to Britain to be the much-loved and respected Secretary to the Scripture Union. He was a great friend of Crusaders and we benefited on several occasions from his helpful advice. He was a man whose deep spirituality was blended with a down-to-earth godly wisdom, all framed in a warm-hearted personality. We remember him with gratitude and thanksgiving.

In the pre-war years the only other Class abroad was in Egypt in Alexandria where there was a British community. It was started in 1925 by Dr Rowland Campion who came to England every summer and will be remembered by some as the ever popular, jolly and warm-hearted 'Docco' at numerous Felixstowe camps. At the piano he would regularly lead excited campers in his 'signature song' – if there is such a thing – entitled: 'Mary had a William goat'. Incidentally he was dentist to the King of Egypt!

In June 1939 a flourishing Class was started in the boarding school of the China Inland Mission at Cheefoo, but alas, it came to an end with the invasion of China by the Japanese. The names of the Leaders of that Class will evoke memories in the minds of some readers, they were S Houghton, H J Chalkey, G P Welch, S G Martin, and D Bentley-Taylor.

After World War II many Crusaders, on leaving the armed services, found employment abroad particularly in the Colonies, and soon there were sizeable ex-patriot groups of British families. Their children with nothing special to do on a Sunday afternoon, were ideal material for Crusaders and, where appropriate, Classes were started. By 1946 there were groups in Cairo,

Jerusalem and in Nugent School, Loka, in the Sudan. Two years later there were flourishing Classes in Nairobi and in Santiago, and a year later at Bethlehem, Bulawayo and two classes in Salisbury (Zimbabwe).

Sadly all these groups gradually came to an end as the countries concerned became independent and many of the ex-patriots returned to Britain or moved elsewhere. However, today Crusaders' international work is extending and there are groups in several countries.

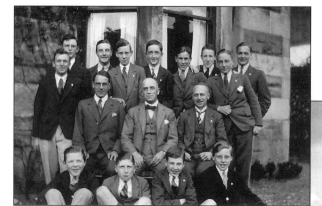

Glasgow South Crusaders in 1927 . . .

. . . and on a walk in 1931

Newton Mearns Crusaders in the 30's

13

OVER THE BORDER AND BEYOND

Towards the end of the twenties, a number of Christian men in Glasgow began to recognise a situation similar to that which had existed in England more than twenty years earlier. Among those concerned to meet the need was the CSSM's full-time representative in Scotland J E Duncan. Jimmy, as he was affectionately known, knew all about Crusaders and he, with the help of T R Murray, decided to start a Class in Kelvindale, which he called Glasgow West; it was officially recognised in September 1927, and this was followed a month later by a Class called Glasgow South under the leadership of John Eaton and Stephen Cox. Another month later Glasgow Hillhead came into being led by S S Taylor and Quintin Carr, then a student at the Bible Training Institute and later, apart from the War years, a much loved staff member of the CSSM in India and the United Kingdom, and a keen supporter of Crusaders all his life.

In the November of that same year the Class called Edinburgh South came into being, followed by Edinburgh Central two months later and Aberdeen the following September. It was tremendously encouraging, for by March 1929 Scotland had a membership of two hundred, while the Union's total membership was more than nine thousand in one hundred and thirty Classes.

In those days the annual statistics indicated the number of: 'Past and present members engaged in outside Christian Work' and the figure reported as at March 1929 was 1507. The Holy Spirit was beginning to do something very remarkable; here were young men, many of whom had come to know the grace of God in Christ while in Crusader Classes, who were now rejoicing in His love and forgiveness and, having been taught the basic Biblical doctrines in Crusaders, were concerned to make His love and forgiveness known to others, and to glorify God in their lives. Learners still but 'able to teach others also'.

We gave up counting long ago, but the total number, known only to God, must be many, many thousands. Over the years, again and again I have met scores of Christian men active in the Lord's service only to discover, often quite by chance that, under God, they owed their conversion and early spiritual development to the faithful ministry and loving care of their respective Crusader Leaders, whom they remembered with heartfelt gratitude. Thankfully I count myself among their number. To God must be all the glory and the praise; to us the privilege of being co-workers together with Him in a wonderfully fruitful field.

Reverting to the progress North of the Border, the Committee in London felt it would be desirable for Scottish affairs to be handled by a Scottish Sub-Committee. The idea found acceptance to the Leaders concerned and in June 1928 the proposal was formally approved and the Sub-Committee held its first meeting on 13th September. When a few days later the minutes of that meeting were read and approved by the General Committee, it was decided to send a gift of £10 as a welcoming gesture and to help the Sub-Committee on its way.

Herbert A Stewart was Scotland's first Hon Secretary and Treasurer, followed by John Eaton in 1936, and then by Norman Wright in 1951, by which time there were seventeen Classes with a membership of over 800.

In October 1927 Ireland came on the Crusader scene with the election of a Class in Belfast under the leadership of F R W Andrews, to be joined a year later by Dick Paisley. Here too the method and ethos of Crusaders was ideal for those youngsters for whom Sunday School had lost its appeal, and by 1951 there were twelve Classes from as far afield as Cork, Dublin and Londonderry, where the much loved T S Mooney was Leader, and the total membership was more than 550.

Checking the above statistics has reminded me how, in those days, the challenge of the overseas Mission Field was strong and demanding. I recall well the general attitude among evangelicals that if you had no specific reason for remaining in Britain, then it was your duty to offer for missionary service overseas. Many Crusaders responded and every so often we had Valedictory Meetings in London to say farewell to those about to set sail, to hear their testimonies, to commend them to God and to present them with a suitably inscribed, leather bound Bible, the cover of which had been embossed in gold with the Crusader crest.

We invariably included an up-to-date list of 'Crusaders on the Overseas Mission Field' in the Annual Reports which indicated the countries in which the Crusaders were working, the missionary societies to which they belonged and the Crusader Classes of which they had been members.

I have just turned up the list published in 1953 which records that in Africa there were 83 Crusader missionaries, in China 9, in Singapore and Malaya 4, in Thailand 1, in India 28, in Pakistan 2, in South America 17, in British

Castlerock Crusader Camp, Northern Ireland, in 1934. Seated in the centre of the photo is "TS" Mooney.

Honduras 1, in Egypt 3, in Burma 4, in Iran 2, in Aden 2, in Palestine 2, in Japan 4, in Indonesia 1, a total of 163.

I have no idea what the number would be today but I well recall my concern to discover whether God wanted me overseas!

Perhaps this is the point where a little autobiography is permissible. Having left Highgate School in 1929 (yes, Mr Vereker had been there too!), I was working for the Anglo-Persian Oil Company (now British Petroleum) and was expecting to go to Persia in due course; was that to be my life's work? Deep down I longed to spend my days in something more worthwhile, although I much enjoyed playing cricket and badminton for the Company and football for the Old Cholmeleians in the winter!

In most lunch hours, there was time to walk down Moorgate to St Margaret's Church in Lothbury, just behind the Bank of England, where I could read my Bible and wait upon God in prayer. I'm not given to strange experiences but on one occasion a verse of Scripture seemed to speak to me personally in a quite definite way. It seemed as if the Holy Spirit was answering my concern regarding my life's work, and it brought peace of mind. That verse became my sheet anchor then and has remained so ever since; it was Ephesians 2:10 'For we are His workmanship, created in Christ Jesus unto good works, which God has before ordained that we should walk in them'.

Although still under 21 years of age, I was an elected Leader of the Muswell Hill Class to which I had been taken by my brother in 1919, when I was eight years old. There nurtured by loving Leaders, faith in Christ as Saviour and Lord gradually became a reality and the challenge to discipleship accepted.

In due course I and several other seniors were invited to assist Jack Hoare, one of the Leaders, in running the Junior Section of the Class; he was a fine character and a brilliant Law student who came out top of all England in his LLB examinations. His devotion to Crusaders was such that before long our meeting place could not accommodate everyone and the Junior Section was moved to a school some distance away. There we continued growing and I well recall the Sunday when our record attendance was 83 Juniors.

Having gained his degree, Jack Hoare promptly left us in order to train for the mission field and he arranged for his mantle to fall on me - hence my youthful election; it was a challenging experience. During this time I was helping to run an evening service for children at a mission in the slums of Islington. It seemed right to balance working among the more privileged in Muswell Hill, with service among the less privileged in and around Pentonville Road. The question of discipline presented very few problems among Crusaders, but at the Mission with up to two hundred noisy boys and girls, you only received the attention you deserved. If you could hold their interest, all was well - lose their interest, and chaos reigned. It was a marvellous training ground for us workers; I'm not sure how much the children got out of it!

It was very hurtful to see so much real poverty: children poorly clothed and sometimes without shoes or socks. When visiting their homes one needed to know not only their addresses but also the number of knocks, for there would be a family on each floor. One knock meant the basement, two knocks, the ground floor, and so on. Although few of those families ever went to church, almost all the parents had attended a Sunday School in their youth, knew the Ten Commandments, also many of the Gospel stories, and firmly believed in God and a judgement to come. In addition, most had an acceptable code of behaviour and exercised a measure of discipline over their children.

Today in Islington there is very little real poverty, most are adequately clad, all have TV sets, many own cars; the contrast is remarkable and to be welcomed, except that the Ten Commandments are unknown and the idea of God is no longer relevant. In addition the confidence of the past has been replaced by a deep down anxiety at what may happen in this nuclear age; how times have changed!

"Phone call for you Wattie," I was in Britannic House working out the 'cost per ton throughput' at one of our BP refineries but put down my pen and went over to the phone; it was A J Vereker, could I lunch with him. I guessed it was something to do with Crusader camping - my two weeks of holiday were always spent at camp.

We met at a restaurant in Moorgate, found an empty table and gave our orders to the waitress and then imagine my astonishment when he suddenly said, "Jack, will you come and join me at Headquarters? Stephen Cox is leaving, I'd like you to take his place." I loved the Union and all it stood for, but the possibility of working for it full time had never once entered my head. Was this God's answer to my concern for a worthwhile life? Somehow it seemed almost too good to be true, but there were obstacles, for example I was under 21 and so at that time had not 'come of age' and would not wish to go against my father's wishes. In addition I felt some obligation to my employers, after all, they had taught me my job and I was now beginning to be useful, should a Christian walk out on them so soon?

To my surprise these and certain other obstacles presented no problem, but the clear sign from God which I asked Him for, never came. This worried me somewhat - in those days Christians spoke so glibly of 'being led'.

When finally I was interviewed by members of the Committee, I expressed my readiness to join the HQ staff but could not say I had received any Divine guidance; this bothered them not at all and so in 1931 I exchanged a large office in Britannic House, Moorgate for a 'cubby hole' in 4 New Bridge Street and began a service which was to last forty years!

THE CRUSADERS' UNION.

You are invited to attend a

Farewell Meeting

at Sion College, Victoria Embankment,

on Wednesday, 1st July, 1936, at 6.30 p.m. to the following

Crusader Missionaries:

Mr. I Anderson	(Monkton Combe)	CHINA
Mr. A. O. Brand	(Dulwich)	AFRICA
Mr. E. Cooper	(Upper Tooting)	AFRICA
Mr. J. M. Field	(Upper Tooting)	AFRICA
*Rev. M. S. Flint	(East Finchley)	BAFFIN LAND
Rev. H. G. Iliff	(High Barnet)	CHINA
Dr. D. W. S. Kaye	(Eastbourne)	RHODESIA
Mr. R. Kingston	(Ramsgate)	MOROCCO
Mr. D. H. Temple	(Blackheath)	CHINA

Chairman: The Rev. F. Houghton (C.I.M.)

Closing Speaker: The Rev. A. Stuart McNairn, F.R.G.S. (E.U.S.A.)

* Already Sailed.

14

ANNUAL EVENTS

As already mentioned, one of the great advantages of a movement like Crusaders has been the ability to provide exciting and enjoyable events on a scale which a local Sunday School could never contemplate. For example in 1929 plans were made for a visit to the Great Western Railway's Locomotive Works at Swindon. The arrangements had been planned for a 'Crusader Special' train with a party of some six hundred in mind. To everyone's amazement no less than 1970 applications came pouring in and it was necessary to lay on three 'specials' on three different days.

The Great Western Railway authorities took a great interest in the project, it was the largest party they had ever handled and they provided their most famous engine 'King George V' to be the engine on each occasion and some striking speeds for those days were recorded; the boys were thrilled – and so were their Leaders!

The following year saw a similar excursion in 'Crusader Specials' to the Southampton Docks and the opportunity to see over the 'Olympic', one of the largest ocean going liners of its day. On this occasion one of the locomotives had an enormous Crusader badge fitted on the front, thanks to the expertise of the Leaders of the Streatham Class. Thereafter that badge made an annual appearance until the streamlining of engines made it impossible to fit!

As mentioned earlier, the Union was very fortunate in having among its Leaders Cecil J Allen who not only edited the 'Crusader Magazine' but who, because of his employment, was able to be the architect of those fascinating annual excursions by rail and was in a position to secure facilities not normally available to others, and because of his encyclopaedic knowledge of railways, made the most of each project.

Incidentally the daily newspapers always welcomed articles written by him and this enabled him to give excellent publicity to the particular rail service used which their Directors greatly welcomed, for in those days the railways of Britain were run independently and there was considerable rivalry between them.

The first Crusader Excursion – 3rd January 1929. The special train left Paddington at 12.40 pm and ran non-stop to Swindon for a tour of the Great Western Railway works

The year 1931 saw three 'Crusader Specials' to Portsmouth Dockyard to see over three battleships: 'Hood', 'Warspite' and 'Nelson', also the Aircraft Carrier 'Courageous' and Lord Nelson's flagship 'Victory'.

And so year by year, thanks to the organising skill of Cecil Allen, thousands of Crusaders enjoyed a fascinating day of unusual interest. The Annual Report for 1938 contains the following:

'Another annual event of no little popularity is the Union excursion which, on this occasion, took the form of a visit to the 'Queen Mary' at Southampton. Over 1,200 Crusaders found their way on board, and more remarkable still found their way off again without losing some of their number in the labyrinthine corridors of this magnificent ship.

It is a stirring sight to see hundreds of boys representative of many schools, drawn together with the intention of enjoying themselves to the full, and a stirring thought to realise that in a few hours they will be scattered over the length and breadth of the country taking with them unforgettable memories of gigantic liners and huge graving docks.

Those responsible for the excursion are possibly still more stirred by the thought that in a few days time they will be meeting together in their respective Crusader Classes equally intent on grasping to the full the spiritual works of the Creator, and thinking equally earnestly of the unseen Hand at the helm of life, so essential to the steering of a safe and steady course.'

Some older readers may remember that the following year, the excursion was to Cranwell where thanks to another Crusader, the then Wing

Commander P J Wiseman, we were thrilled by a flying display put on for our delight by the RAF; and saw a brand new fighter aircraft called the 'Hawker Hurricane' little guessing what a vital role it would shortly be playing, together with the 'Spitfire', in the defence of Britain.

Cranwell was on a branch line and, on the return journey, as our trains approached the main line at Sleaford Junction, Cecil Allen had arranged for the 'Flying Scotsman', a crack train of its day, to pass by at full speed on its way from Edinburgh to Kings Cross. With magnificent split second timing, hundreds of Crusader train spotters were provided with a thrilling sight they would never forget as the mighty 'beast' thundered past – lucky Crusaders!

A Crusader Special

17th
ANNUAL
SPORTS DAY

(Under A.A.A. Laws)

Saturday, 23rd April, 1938,

at 2.30 p.m.,

at the

LONDON UNIVERSITY
ATHLETIC GROUND,

Motspur Park, New Malden.

Station : MOTSPUR PARK (S.R.), from Waterloo.

Accommodation for Cars and Coaches.

CRUSADERS'
UNION

1978

Jubilee Sports

15

ATHLETIC SPORTS

'The General Committee has decided to hold a Union Sports Day on Saturday, April 29th next. Sir William Lancaster has kindly permitted the use of his grounds on Putney Hill for the Sports' - so ran the announcement in the February number of the 'Crusader Magazine' in 1922, and in doing so introduced an event which ever since has played a significant part in Crusaders' annual activities. What began as a very modest affair in which 33 Classes participated, developed over the years into an event highly regarded in the realm of amateur athletics and which, at its peak, involved more than a thousand Crusader competitors.

After three years at Putney, better facilities were required to cope with increasing numbers and the venue was moved to the London County Athletic Ground at Herne Hill. In those early days the Union Sports owed much to Frank Bray, a Leader of the Highgate Class, and a schoolmaster who knew how to organise and carry through an event of this kind with both speed and efficiency. He always acted as official starter, and an excerpt from a light-hearted account of the 1925 meeting in the May magazine, gives a colourful indication of how he managed to deal with so many participants, it speaks of:

'Hundreds of youths clad in running shorts ... enter Mr Bray plus artillery. Then the guns fired and the runners ran ... the heats were run with such rapidity that many a laggard from heat number one, found himself in the semi-final as the winner of heat number two! And still the guns fired, and still they ran ...!' One interested spectator said he had the strong impression that 'Frank was using a machine gun rather than a starter's pistol'!

Yet again increasing numbers called for greater facilities and in 1932, with entries approaching the five hundred mark, the Sports Meeting was moved to the University of London's Athletic Ground at Motspur Park, which became its home for almost fifty years.

The outbreak of war in 1939 inevitably put an end to major sports meetings, but by 1944 improved conditions prompted two Leaders to plan and organise a South London Sports Meeting at the Tooting Bec Track, and this was repeated in the following two years.

'On your marks, get set, go!'

At Copthall in the 90's

Ian Botham congratulates Tim Pamphlett

The two Leaders concerned were Ralph Naylor of the Upper Tooting Class and Harold Thompson of the West Wickham Class, and it would be hard to exaggerate the value of their influence on the post-war meetings. It was their zeal and foresight that succeeded in securing the interest and practical co-operation from officials in the wider world of athletics. It was their skill and devotion to detail that enabled the Union Sports to get off to a fine start when they recommenced in 1947, and caused the Crusader Sports to be regarded as among the best in their class.

When in due course Ralph Naylor left for Africa, Harold Thompson continued as Hon Sports Secretary serving in that capacity for upwards of thirty years - a marathon indeed! He was followed with equal devotion by Wilf Tyler, a Leader of the Eastwood Class, and then by Dennis Lowden, a Leader of the Golders Green Class, who in 1978 produced an attractive Souvenir Programme to mark the 50th anniversary of the Sports in which, among many interesting details, particular reference was made to two Crusader athletes who achieved international fame.

One was the Rev Tom Farrell of the Liverpool, West Derby Class who represented Great Britain on some twenty-five occasions, took part in two Olympic Games and twice broke the British Record for the 400 metres hurdles.

The other was David Hemery of the Frinton and Colchester Classes, who gained Gold, Silver and Bronze Olympic medals, broke the World Record for the 400 metres hurdles, and in 1968 was voted BBC Sportsman of the Year. Another item of interest was a reference to Throwing the Cricket Ball. In 1969 a young Crusader from the Yeovil Class took part in the Under 13 event and threw the ball 40 feet further than the boy who had created the previous record a year or two earlier. The boy was Ian Botham and his record remained unbeaten until 1993, when Tim Pamphlett, of Maidstone North Crusaders, exceeded Botham's throw of 63.32 metres by more than 5 metres.

Since 1979 events for girls have been included in the programme too and in 1981 the Sports moved North of the Thames to the splendid Copthall Stadium in Hendon where it looks like remaining for the foreseeable future.

16

CONFERENCES

From the earliest days of the Union, day and evening conferences were held from time to time, when papers were read on various aspects of the Union's work, followed by questions and discussion; but in 1927, fifty Leaders gathered for the first time for a residential weekend conference at the Quaker Centre, Old Jordans in Buckinghamshire. It proved to be so worthwhile an occasion that another was held the following year. I still recall the nights in that particular June as the younger members of the conference slept, or rather didn't sleep, on camp beds in a large barn purported to be constructed with timber from the 'Mayflower', the ship which had conveyed the first Quaker settlers to America. But the coldness of the nights contrasted with the warmth of the days as praise and prayer, papers and discussions bound us together in a loving concern to bring more youngsters to Christ and His Cross, in our respective Classes. We went home 'treading on air', rejoicing in our privilege of being entrusted with the Gospel and firmly resolved to put into practice new ideas which the conference had taught us.

Since that time, apart from the War years, Leaders' Conferences have played an important part in the work and sometimes even the Swanwick Centre has been unable to accommodate all who wished to attend. Similar conferences are also held in Scotland and Ireland.

The value of these residential conferences caused the Committee to consider the possibility of experimenting with an Easter Houseparty weekend conference for Senior Crusaders. The Crusader Headmaster of Collington Rise School in Bexhill gladly agreed to provide the accommodation but so great was the demand that an additional school had to be secured in order to cope with the 150 young men who applied. It proved a never-to-be-forgotten experience and became a regular feature of the annual programme in subsequent years but varying the locations, Lancing College one year, Ovingdean School near Brighton another year and so on.

The programme was a full one, mornings were given to doctrinal teaching, Biblical exegesis and devotional sessions. Afternoons were free for games and excursions, while the evenings provided what were called 'Fireside Chats'

The first Leaders' Conference in 1927

Leaders' Conference at High Leigh in 1956

A Swanwick Leaders' Weekend in the 80's

when all kinds of questions relevant to young men, with life before them, were raised and discussed.

The Union had been blessed with two very gifted Leaders who attended many of these Houseparties. They were as different in personality as chalk from cheese but together they provided a fascinating blend of wisdom, helpfulness and humour as, sitting each side of the fire and surrounded by Crusaders, they led the discussion and answered questions with frequent reference to Scripture.

One of those Leaders was Frank Bacon, a warm-hearted quick witted man from the business world; the other was Montague Goodman a precise lawyer, gifted in clear exposition and much sought after as a speaker for Christian Conventions and meetings. Perhaps he did not possess quite such a sense of humour as Frank Bacon, particularly when, on one occasion, he found his pyjamas floating from the top of the school's flagpole!

Many of those privileged to be at those early houseparties looked back on them as the time when faith was firmly established, when the Bible came alive and the joy of the Lord became an inner reality. Most of them returned determined to become Crusader Leaders - many of them did.

17

ANNUAL GENERAL MEETINGS

Crusaders in the 1920s and 1930s were not put off by this rather grandiose title; those whose Classes were within reach of London knew it represented an exciting occasion when two-and-a-half thousand boys would travel with their leaders to the Central Hall, Westminster, to enjoy an inspiring gathering.

Most Classes in the London area itself hired double-decker omnibuses, which were open-topped in earlier days; some Classes needed two such buses to bring their members to Westminster. It was an unusual sight to see dozens of buses parked in and around nearby Tothill Street, many bearing Class names and some sporting large Crusader badges.

The only exception, at this time, was in 1936 when the Albert Hall was used once again, to celebrate the thirtieth anniversary of the Union's founding - this time carefully respecting the Hall's ticket regulations!

In due course the idea of an annual get together was taken up by some of the provincial Classes, those from the midlands gathered in Leicester; the northern Classes in Manchester, the Scottish Classes in Edinburgh and Glasgow, and the Irish Classes in Belfast.

With the passing of the years, the programme for each AGM grew more sophisticated with the introduction of special features to illustrate a spiritual theme. On one occasion ultra-violet light was used in a most intriguing way to reveal what previously had been invisible: bear in mind there was no television in those days utilising costly visual tricks! On another occasion a giant Crusader badge was put together piece by piece with appropriate explanation and comment. Another time, the model of a giant battleship was the centrepiece for a talk on the Christian's voyage through life and the Devil's devious strategies designed to cause disaster. Yet another occasion saw a Roman soldier gradually being equipped with his armour, his helmet, his shield and his sword, once again with Ephesians 6 in mind.

In due course advancing technology provided an additional item which quickly became a regular 'must'. At Headquarters we purchased a 16 mm cine-camera, and year by year, at first in black and white and then in improving colour, it was possible to present a half-hour film of all the main

Thirty Years After!

JUBILEE RALLY PROGRAMME
THE CRUSADERS' UNION

1906 - 1956

LOOKING UNTO JESUS Hebrews 12 v 2

Chairman: Lieut.-Gen. Sir Arthur E. Smith, K.C.B., K.B.E. ... ... President
At the Organ: Mr. Cecil J. Allen, F.R.C.O. ... ... Hon. Treasurer
Conductor of Choir: Mr. Brian Howard ... ...

Before the Rally

6.5 to 6.20 p.m. Recital on the Organ by Mr. Brian S. Howard
6.20 to 6.30 p.m. Community Singing : Organ Improvisations : Community Chorus by Mr. Cecil J. Allen

Order of Service

National Anthem

Hymn

Invocation & Prayer
Mr. Herbert Bevington
(Vice-President)

The President Speaks
Lieut.-Gen.
Sir Arthur E. Smith

1 O praise ye the Lord !
Praise Him in the height ;
Rejoice in His Word,
Ye angels of light ;
Ye heavens, adore Him
By Whom ye were made,
And worship before Him
In brightness arrayed.

2 O praise ye the Lord !
Praise Him upon earth :
In tuneful accord,
Ye sons of new birth ;
Praise Him Who hath brought you
His grace from above,
Praise Him Who hath taught you
To sing of His love.

Tune : Laudate Dominum

3 O praise ye the Lord,
All things that give sound ;
Each jubilant chord
Re-echo around !
Loud organs, His glory
Tell forth in deep tone,
And, sweet harp, the story
Of what He hath done.

4 O praise ye the Lord !
Thanksgiving and song
To Him be outpoured
All ages along ;
For love in creation,
For heaven restored,
For grace of salvation,
O praise ye the Lord !

The **ROYAL ALBERT HALL**

SATURDAY 14th APRIL, 1956

30 Years After – Albert Hall Rally

Union events from the previous twelve months, together with a spoken commentary. There on the giant screen, Crusaders could relive the Athletic Sports at Motspur Park, or the Excursions in those special trains to exciting places like Southampton Docks or the Railway Works at Crewe or to Cranwell and the RAF. Of course the Summer Camps, Houseparties and Expeditions came in for considerable film coverage, providing for some, the additional thrill of actually seeing themselves on the screen. Each film then became available for Rallies in the Provinces and Classes were often glad to use them at local events such as Birthday Squashes or Parents' Receptions. In due course, thanks to Murray Thomsett, a Crusader who worked for the BBC, some excellent sound films were produced in a highly professional manner.

In due course AGMs gave way to Camp Rallies in the Christmas holidays when the complete facilities of the Central Hall, Westminster were used for a reunion of campers who had participated in the previous summer's programme.

First there would be a grand get-together in the large hall with an entertaining programme culminating in a film shot at many of the Camp sites and which revived campers' memories of the thrilling times they had experienced together under canvas, or on expeditions abroad, or in houseparties.

This was followed by tea in Camp groups when old friendships could be renewed, and finally together again in the large hall to sing the familiar choruses and to listen to a talk, usually aimed at encouraging the many who had made a commitment to Christ during Camp and who were probably finding the Christian life a lot tougher than they had expected.

18

KEEPING IN TOUCH

Each year a considerable number of senior Crusaders go on to University, the majority in pre-war years to Oxford, Cambridge or London. The Annual Report for 1934 records the fact that there were 80 Crusaders at Oxford, 100 at Cambridge and 70 at London. Although their own Class Leaders would usually keep in touch with these undergraduates, the General Committee decided that Headquarters should also maintain contact, and for several good reasons.

For many it would be the first time they had lived away from home, and loneliness could be a problem for some initially. In addition it was important to try and link them on to their University Christian Union, which was part of the Inter-Varsity Fellowship, for there they would find a warm welcome, and an atmosphere similar to that of their Crusader Class; in fact many of its members would be Crusaders.

With all this in mind, squashes were held at the beginning of each academic year at the above Universities when 'freshers' could meet Crusaders already experienced by at least a year of University life and who, in addition to offering friendship, were in a position to give advice regarding the numerous societies which would endeavour to recruit the newcomer. But there was more to it than that. These young men now had long Summer vacations and many of them were just the sort required as officers at Crusader Camps. They would be told of the need and invited to help the following Summer.

Then looking further ahead, when they had obtained their degrees, many would probably leave home to commence their careers elsewhere. If they should go to places where Crusader Classes already existed, the respective Leaders would be informed so that early contact could be made and the new-comer given a warm welcome; for here was potential leadership material, and sometimes a very real answer to prayer.

Should the graduate go to a Crusader-less place, this could be the first step in the formation of a new Class. Now there are Colleges and Universities all over the United Kingdom and Head Office still seeks to maintain contact, through the post, with Crusader students and to link them with Christian Unions through the UCCF, for the needs and the opportunities are greater than ever.

When a senior Crusader left his Class to take up some active Christian service, often in his local Church, (or if he felt he had outgrown the Class) the last thing he wanted was to lose touch with his contemporaries who were also leaving or had already left for similar reasons, or with his friends still in the Class.

With this in mind, and also to enable Crusaders from nearby Classes who were in a similar position to meet one another, 'Crusader Fellowships' were formed in suitable areas. These Fellowships met at regular intervals, most were monthly, and usually on a weeknight evening. The programme would normally comprise refreshments, plenty of opportunity for conversation and finally a devotional session and a visiting speaker.

Most Fellowships had membership cards which would indicate dates of meetings, also the names of the visiting speakers and the subjects to be dealt with. All older Crusaders were encouraged to attend, but actual membership of a Fellowship was effected by the giving of a brief testimony to a personal faith in Christ as Saviour and Lord, when the opportunity to do so was given during the devotional session. For many of us it was the first occasion on which we plucked up sufficient courage to testify in public and it meant a great deal, particularly to those with shy dispositions. By 1938 there were 23 such groups in various parts of the UK and they met a real need.

A further item under this 'Keeping in Touch' heading, the value and importance of which it would be hard to over-estimate, has been mentioned earlier: Associate Membership for former Crusaders and leaders who long that the blessings and joy which they experience in Crusaders might be made available to the young people of today and so continue to support the work.

It is my hope that some past members reading this history, who have not previously considered Associate Membership, will wish to do so now. They can be assured of a warm welcome.

19

OTHER SHEEP

In 1926, the Headquarters of a construction company was moved from Carlisle to London. The owner of that company decided to set up home in Mill Hill in North London and in less than a year he had joined the leadership of the Mill Hill Crusader Class - his name was John Laing.

Who could have guessed that the name, then virtually unknown outside Carlisle, would one day be recognised worldwide as representing a firm of high repute and integrity, employing thousands of men capable of tackling the most challenging of construction work; selected to build the initial section of Britain's first motorway - the M1, and chosen to rebuild blitzed Coventry Cathedral. The story of John Laing's firm's achievements seems never ending.

A robust Christian, and yet a man of great simplicity and gentle humility, John Laing's greatest joy was to tell others of the Saviour he loved and served. Never a man to do things by halves, he found in Crusaders a movement after his own heart and, in one way and another he served and supported the Union for the remainder of his very long life.

For many years he never missed camping with Crusaders, sometimes as Commandant, sometimes as Padre. He played all the games with great zest; the boys loved him and many would share their problems with him, somehow his simple genuineness evoked their confidence.

He readily made his firm's expertise and resources available when something special was required such as for a Rally in the Central Hall, Westminster. On one occasion, as mentioned previously, providing a specially constructed, very large and lifelike warship so enabling the speaker, a much loved Leader, Bill Sharpe, to draw

Sir John Laing

87

spiritual lessons from his experiences as an officer in the Navy during the War. On another occasion we were provided with scaffolding which reached from the floor to the ceiling and, from this it was possible to make a simulated parachute jump. The speaker on this occasion was Paul Rowden, Leader of the Danbury Class, who during the war had been a paratrooper. Can you imagine the thrill as he spoke from the top of the scaffolding, on the practical reality of faith under fire and then proceeded to jump off!

It wasn't long before some of the more daring Crusaders present were jumping off too! An object lesson never to be forgotten.

John Laing worshipped with the Open Brethren and he decided to build a meeting place in nearby Burnt Oak. Woodcroft Evangelical Church, as it is called, was opened in January 1928. Before long a Sunday School was started which quickly numbered several hundred. It was heavy going, for most of the children came from the nearby London County Council estate and discipline was a real problem, particularly among the older boys. It was natural for John Laing to wonder if the way Crusaders were run would go some way towards tackling the problem, and he shared his thoughts with others in the fellowship who were concerned to find a suitable answer to the challenge.

They agreed that whatever plan was decided on, it must have a prayerful basis and there must also be a close link between Leaders and boys. Again like Crusaders there must be a badge which would be a privilege to wear and won by regular attendance. The name decided on for the group was thought to be very important, avoiding any association with 'school', so Sunday School was definitely out.

They chose the name 'Covenanter Band' and John Laing's biography tells how: 'After a false start of a month or two, John Laing offered to claim release

Covenanter Badge

for two years from the Mill Hill Crusaders, and to devote his efforts to the new venture, helped by William Sivey and a young assistant, Roland Webb.'

The biography goes on to say: 'Roland Webb heard from John Cansdale, a friend in Rugby whom he had not seen for some years: the letter brought the information that Cansdale was running a similar boys' work in connection with a Brethren church there, under the name Covenanters.'

They decided to associate and since those days the Covenanter Union has gone ahead on broadly similar lines to Crusaders, but always positively linked with the youth work of a local church, which takes the initiative and responsibility for forming groups and appointing leaders. In this way the

Covenanter group enjoys all the benefits of belonging to a movement capable of providing facilities and activities far greater than it would be possible for the local church to supply.

Crusaders has always enjoyed a warm and happy relationship with Covenanters, in fact quite a number of their Leaders and members of their Council have been Crusaders. It is gratifying to know that those who founded the movement, looked to Crusaders for a method and a pattern which has served them well in a mostly non-conformist church situation.

Some years later, in 1935 to be precise, a young curate in charge of the new Church of Emmanuel, Tolworth, which was located in a fast developing housing estate, felt concern for the children in his Sunday School who had nothing to go on to when they reached secondary school age. It is recorded that: 'He felt that it was vitally important to provide a vehicle which would present Christ to the teenagers in an attractive manner. Also he felt that there was a need for a group which had an evangelical, Anglican emphasis and teaching. That young curate was the Rev (now Canon) Herbert Taylor, and he sensed that God was speaking to him about the youngsters in his Church.' He decided the vehicle in question must have a meaningful name, and at that time there was a Christian magazine run by one Roger de Pemberton, a friend of his (and incidentally an old Crusader); the name of the magazine was 'Pathfinder' and with permission gladly given, Herbert Taylor decided to call his new group 'Pathfinders'.

The next necessity was the now familiar badge, shaped like a shield with the

St Andrew's Cross and the four symbols in each segment. Some of these badges were ready for the very first meeting on 6th October 1935 when a dozen boys and girls were present.

Other Anglican Churches, seeing the success of Canon Taylor's initiative, decided to follow his example and by 1953 there were about twenty groups called 'Pathfinders',

Pathfinder Badge mainly in the South of England. About this time an old Crusader, Canon Tom Livermore was Vicar of Morden; he had a Pathfinder group and he felt there was a great need in the Church of England for anofficially recognised youth movement, and urged that Pathfinders should 'go nationwide'. So it was that the movement came under the wing of 'The Church Society' and one of Canon Livermore's curates, the Rev Richard Bowdler, became Pathfinder's first Secretary.

I well recall a visit from Richard at this time: he wanted to discuss everything Crusaders did, and how they did it. We gladly gave him all the help we could, together with copies of our literature and, in the years that followed, rejoiced to see the way the movement forged ahead, doing for Anglicanism what Covenanters was doing for non-conformists.

They now have all those extras which help to make a youth movement popular including summer camps, introduced in the first place at the instigation of the Rev Keith Weston, then a curate at Emmanuel Northwood, and yes, another Crusader! Over the years quite a number of Pathfinder Leaders have been Crusaders. Incidentally the movement now comes under the aegis of the Church Pastoral Aid Society.

20

GATHERING STORM CLOUDS

We looked anxiously across the Channel towards Continental Europe and wondered sometimes fearfully, sometimes hopefully. Chamberlain had come back from his meeting with Hitler in September 1938 and, at the airport, had held aloft as if in triumph, the piece of paper which Hitler had signed. "Peace in our time!" he had exclaimed, but most doubted; particularly as plans were made for everyone to be provided with a gas mask and, in addition, material was made available to enable families to construct their own 'Anderson' air-raid shelters in their gardens.

Hoping against hope we went ahead with our plans for the Summer Camps and Houseparties of 1939 even though Hitler's Panzer Divisions were continuing their relentless advances and once again the lights were going out all over Europe.

We usually ran two camps and two houseparties in succession at each location and the first ones were carried through successfully. I was at the second houseparty at Bembridge School on the Isle of Wight and we were having a great time. Suddenly there was a phone call from Mr Vereker at Headquarters, "Send all the boys home at once, get one or two officers to stay and help you clear things up and then go on to the Thurlestone Camp in Devon, they have all gone home; get the tents and equipment back to Smiths, the hirers." We were at war!

That night there was a heavy thunderstorm and at first, as we looked out to sea, we were not sure whether the vivid flashes were from heaven or from Hitler! Having cleared up at Bembridge, Gordon Buchanan, a Leader of the Upper Tooting Class, kindly drove me down to Thurlestone in Devon where together we dealt with clearing the camp site and, a day or two later, we returned to London. It's not possible to convey on paper the feelings of tense anxiety which somehow pervaded the capital. The last war with its bitter memories of privation, bloodshed and loss, was little more than twenty years previous; must it happen all over again and this time on a far greater scale? It was generally assumed that London would be decimated by bombing - the outlook was grim.

General Committee during World War II
Left to right: Back row – Alan Farrin, Colin Waldram, Oliver Gilbart Smith
Middle row – John Laing, D M Miller, Reg Silvester, Harold Keay, Gordon Humphreys, J B Langford
Front row – Jack Miller, John Vereker, Herbert Bevington, Frank Bacon, Laurence Head

Postcard from a Prisoner of War

It was about midday that I climbed the stairs at No 4 New Bridge Street and on entering the HQ Office was met by John Spencer, our young and somewhat cheeky Office Boy. I greeted him and his reply was, "You've got the sack!" I smiled at what I assumed was one of his jokes but this time he appeared serious as he insisted, "It's true, you've got the sack!" Puzzled, I put down the items I was carrying and went in to see Mr Vereker. "What's all this about getting the sack; I've just been talking to Spencer?" Mr Vereker looked serious. "I was wondering how to tell you," he said, "I'm very sorry. The General Purposes Sub-Committee had an emergency meeting yesterday and, in view of the situation, decided they cannot guarantee your salary after the end of the year; they will quite understand if you decide to leave and join up before then."

Committees are 'funny' things; they can sometimes take decisions as a group which the members, as individuals, would scarcely even contemplate. In this case, here was a Sub-Committee trying to cope with an emergency in an atmosphere of severe panic. It seemed an unkind and hurtful decision and it grieved me greatly, after all I was the Assistant Secretary and had served the Union for nine years; however, looking back I can say, as Joseph did, 'but God meant it for good'. Less than six weeks later I was at the RAF station, Little

Rissington, in the Cotswolds as an 'Acting Pilot Officer on probation' doing PT and square-bashing at seven o'clock in the morning, and so began six years of active service mostly spent dealing with ammunition and explosives, some of the time in Burma of all places – what a contrast!

Crusader Headquarters was moved, as a temporary measure to 43 Parade Mansions in Hendon, North London, where Mr Vereker and his secretary did their best to continue serving the Union. By 1941 thirty-four Classes had suspended operations, often as a result of the evacuation of children to safer areas or the call-up of Leaders for the Armed Forces. By now there were about 1,500 Leaders and seniors in the three Services and every effort was being made to keep in touch with them by means of a monthly Newsletter, the Magazine and Scripture Union notes.

This link meant a great deal to its recipients, and in addition lists were included from time to time containing the names and addresses of Leaders and other Christian folk who would be pleased to offer hospitality to Crusaders in the Forces.

Only those who have known what it is like, in the uncertain atmosphere of war, to be suddenly forced to live in an environment that is unfamiliar and tough, and in a situation generally hostile to Christian standards, can appreciate the blessing of an hour or two spent in the warm welcoming atmosphere of a godly home. Frequently such hospitality included a meal, although such generosity could evoke pangs of conscience as one remembered their meagre rations compared with the amount of food normally provided to servicemen in camp. Nor was the hospitality list limited to addresses in the United Kingdom. I still recall the thrill of discovering the home of a Crusader in Calcutta, the warmth of his welcome, and the sight of friendly little lizards climbing up the lounge wall, catching mosquitos and other unwelcome insects!

Wherever the various postings took me in those six years of war, I was nearly always able to make contact with Crusaders. Perhaps the most memorable occasion was when I was posted to the Far East and joined the S S Orontes in the Clyde prior to setting off in convoy; the very first person I met, as I climbed aboard, was Esmond Broad, a Leader of the Putney Class and before long a small group of Christians was able to meet every day for prayer and Bible study as we zig-zagged about the Atlantic avoiding German submarines.

During this time there was still an average of 5,000 Crusaders meeting in their Classes on Sunday afternoons. Camps were no longer possible but instead Summer Houseparties began to be organised. At first there were two at Mostyn House School, Parkgate, Cheshire and one at Ludgrove School,

Jack Watford, Assistant Secretary 1931-1946 and
General Secretary 1946-1976

Wokingham, Berkshire. As the war trailed on, every effort was needed to provide the nation's food, and so, instead of a programme full of games, part of each day was devoted to helping local farmers gather their crops. Some readers will recall the Government's call and slogan 'DIG FOR VICTORY' - some Crusaders found themselves digging for potatoes!

By 1942, Headquarters was in postal touch with nearly two thousand Crusaders in the Forces and already more than sixty were known to have been killed. The records tell of more than forty decorations for gallantry including two awards of the Victoria Cross. Also at this time there were at least thirty-five Crusaders in prisoner-of-war camps in Italy, Malaya, Singapore and Algeria.

Alas this was only the beginning; by 1944 there were upwards of four thousand Crusaders in one or other of the three Services and, in addition, others were serving on the Home Front in, for example, the Fire Service. In due course in the South of England, air raids gave way to the threat of flying bombs, nicknamed 'doodle bugs' – it was a nerve racking experience to hear the 'pop-pop' of their engines and to watch the approaching menaces knowing that those engines would suddenly cut out, causing the bombs to plummet to earth creating death and destruction. Later the flying bombs gave way to rockets which provided no advance warning of their coming for the rockets arrived first and the sound of their coming followed after; they caused even greater destruction.

At long last the end of the war, at least in Europe, came in sight and the Union's Wartime Committee began to give serious thought to plans for the future. The 257 Classes of pre-war days with an average attendance of about 10,000 had diminished to 224 Classes with an average attendance of around 5,000; there was much to be done as the prospect of peace became a reality. In particular the Butler Education Act of 1944 had introduced fundamental changes to the basis of education in Britain. Until now Crusaders had catered mainly for boys from public, secondary and private schools for whom Sunday Schools had little attraction; it was thought that perhaps the new Act would open the way to greater opportunities, and the Committee was alert to the challenge.

It came at long last – 'unconditional surrender' in Europe and Hitler dead. VE day had arrived! Somehow it seemed remote and unreal as, seated in a bamboo hut in the jungle, some of us gathered round a very crackly radio set listening to a re-broadcast by 'All India Radio' of the news from London – even the sound of cheering crowds outside Buckingham Palace gave a sense of fantasy, for our war with Japan must go on; perhaps now we would be getting the supplies we so much needed, VJ day still seemed a long way off. It came much sooner than expected with the dropping of the bomb and the horror of Hiroshima and Nagasaki; the atomic age had dawned, and with it, peace.

Demobilisation was dealt with on a 'first in, first out' basis and soon I was taking my last look at the Burma jungle as we flew out from Rangoon and over the Bay of Bengal on the first leg of the journey home. It was December 1945 and the Minutes of the meeting of the General Committee in January 1946 record the decision to invite me to rejoin the Headquarters' staff, once again as Assistant Secretary – but I wasn't too sure; the summary treatment in 1939 had not been forgotten and I was now a married man. In addition Mr Vereker was far from well, wounds sustained in World War I were taking their toll. He had not been the easiest of colleagues to work with in pre-war days and now with the experiences and responsibilities of the war behind me, it might not be quite so easy to accept his extremely strongly held views and attitudes without question. In addition I had been urged by several of the padres I had assisted on active service, to apply for Anglican ordination, and I had been invited to attend a selection board conference at Cuddesdon College near Oxford.

The General Committee explained to me that Mr Vereker was about to have an operation on his eyes in an endeavour to correct his double vision and hopefully alleviate his constant headaches, and they pressed me to help them out at Headquarters. I offered them my 'de-mob' leave of some months which they were glad to accept, while fully appreciating my concern to try to discover God's will for the future. Soon the selection board conference came and went and afterwards I received a strong recommendation to train for the Anglican ministry with the promise - unusual in pre-war days - that my financial needs would be met during training.

I rested on my favourite verse of Scripture (Ephesians 2:10) and was soon happily immersed in the task of rebuilding the Union and planning the future in joyful fellowship with the Committee and Sub-Committees. Among other things we were seeking a suitable memorial to the upwards of six hundred Crusaders whose lives had been lost during the conflict. Some of them had left their modest savings to the Union and quite a number of bereaved parents decided to give the movement money left to them by their sons, because Crusaders had meant so much to them as they grew to manhood.

The total sum in the Memorial Fund was a little over five hundred pounds and it was suggested that this would be enough to purchase and equip a suitable field as a permanent camp site. I well recall the reaction of John Laing when this proposal was put forward at one of the weekly lunch-time meetings of the General Purposes Sub-Committee, "Oh no, surely we can do better than that, these fellows have given their lives for us; will you allow me to look for something more appropriate?" Members readily agreed and during the months that followed he sought, through agents, to find a place which would meet the specification he had in mind. It had to be located in an attractive and secluded setting and be close to the sea, affording safe bathing. It must be suitable for a camp site and perhaps provide facilites for a conference centre - altogether a far more ambitious plan than anyone else had considered possible. One day in April 1947, Mr Laing asked Mr Bevington, our General Committee chairman, and me to accompany him to the Isle of Wight - perhaps he had at last found the place. He took us to a gentleman's estate near Seaview whose place of business was in Portsmouth; he evidently had another property on the mainland and this place was simply his summer residence.

The main entrance was through a pair of magnificent wrought iron gates which opened on to a gravel drive of a hundred yards or so, and there round a bend was a fair-sized house with a quite imposing pillared entrance at the top of a flight of steps. Around the house were well-kept gardens, beyond which were meadows, an orchard, a gardener's cottage and through the trees, the sea - just five minutes' walk down the lane which bordered the 28 acre estate.

The house itself consisted of rooms occupied by the family and, behind the green baize-covered door, the completely self-contained servants' quarters. There were also several sizeable storerooms and a large basement. The more we looked, the more thrilled we became; here was scope exactly in line with what Mr Laing had in mind - a marvellous camp site, a house capable of adaptation into a conference centre - and all in a beautiful and secluded setting close to the sea. The name of the house was 'Westbrook'.

The Minutes of the General Committee meeting on 15th April 1947 make interesting reading, members had been provided with full details of the property and both Mr Laing and Mr Bevington said they regarded the place as ideal for the purpose in mind. Mr Laing said he thought the price would be about £15,000 of which he would expect the Union to provide £5,000. The members 'expressed their most sincere and deep sense of gratitude to Mr Laing for his love for the Union in making this magnanimous offer'.

During the discussion that followed it was appreciated that increased sleeping accommodation would be necessary if the conference part of the project were to be financially viable. In addition the fact of being located on the island meant that weekend or casual visitors might be deterred from using the place.

Mr Laing was anxious that members should be completely free, if they wished to seek a suitable place on the mainland, his offer was not tied to any particular property. In order to give members time to consider the matter prayerfully, it was decided to hold a special meeting of the Committee on 8th May 1947 by which time some other members would have visited the property. At that meeting after a lengthy discussion it was agreed to ask Mr Laing to open negotiations 'with a view to acquiring Westbrook House and Estate'.

Mr Laing, with typical zeal, acted very quickly and at the next meeting of the Committee less than two weeks later he announced that the house and

Westbrook, near Seaview, Isle of Wight, in the early 70s

Enjoying the Swimming Pool at Westbrook

grounds had been secured for £10,800, which included the ground rent from three small cottages on a corner of the estate.

Everyone was thrilled and a Sub-Committee comprising Messrs Bevington, R W Ewan and A A T Farrin was appointed to: 'plan the development of Westbrook for the purpose intended'. Mr Laing allowed himself to be co-opted 'for as long a period as his many other duties would permit'. Actually Mr Laing loved Westbrook and he remained an active member of the Sub-Committee for very many years. In fact, the last Camp he ever attended as an officer, was there – his great joy was to know that it had become the spiritual birthplace of literally hundreds of boys – it continues to be so – what a fitting memorial to those Crusaders who died fighting for our freedom from tyranny.

During the period following the purchase, it was a joy to find so many Leaders whose business interests could provide some of the many items required to change a private house into a conference centre; things like blankets and beds, and in particular in the kitchen area which soon had the most modern facilities through the generosity of Mr Ernest Bartlett, a Leader of the Golders Green Class, whose firm manufactured some of the best culinary equipment in Britain.

During this time Mr Vereker was away, at first in hospital where the operation on his eyes was performed, and then, following advice from his specialist that he should have a long period of complete rest, he was able to go with Mrs Vereker to the West Indies, thanks once again to the generosity of Mr Laing. On his returning to England, he went to see his specialist who said he must give up any idea of returning to desk and office work, and recommended a more open air occupation. Mr Vereker's reaction was immediate, "It's Westbrook for me," and so it was; the Committee readily appointed him the first Warden of our new island centre – it was the ideal answer to his problem and mine; he never came back to Crusader Headquarters, and I never left!

Among his many gifts Mr Vereker was very practical and so he was an ideal person to deal with the adaptation of Westbrook. The Sub-Committee was enlarged and Mr Cecil Allen became its most energetic chairman, in which capacity he served for more than twenty years; his facility for free travel on the railway enabled him to keep in close touch with the work there; he was a frequent visitor and a welcome supporter and adviser.

The Minutes of the General Committee dated 20th April 1948 contain the following:

'Westbrook. Mr Allen reported on two very successful Easter Houseparties which had tested the Westbrook machinery and had proved it to be thoroughly satisfactory from every point of view. Attention was drawn to the Dedication Service planned for 29th May and he hoped that members would be free to attend.'

On 29th May a number of us gathered at midday outside the main entrance to the house. Mrs Laing had been invited to participate in a brief ceremony to mark the official opening of Westbrook. It was intended that Air Commodore P J Wiseman, General Committee Chairman at that time, would address a few words of gratitude to Mr and Mrs Laing and would then ask Mrs Laing to turn the key, cross the threshold and pronounce Westbrook open.

As Air Commodore Wiseman began to speak the heavens suddenly opened in a manner worthy of a tropical monsoon; we all rushed for cover and Mrs Laing with great presence of mind quickly turned the key and entered the hall followed by everyone else – I guess it was the fastest official opening on record – someone suggested that Westbrook had certainly received its baptism!

Having toured the building, lunch was provided and afterwards there was a very moving ceremony in the meeting room when Westbrook was formally

Book of Remembrance at Westbrook

dedicated, a bronze memorial plaque was unveiled, and a Roll of Honour, in beautifully bound book form, was presented. The Roll was inscribed with the names, together with their respective Classes, of all Crusaders known to have died serving King and Country during the War. I shall never forget the gentle tears of the Crusader Leader who performed the act of unveiling that plaque – he had lost his only son. The closing address was given by the Rev Guy H King, one of the founding fathers of the Union. The plaque and Roll of Honour are there at Westbrook for all to see, the latter in a glass case; a page is turned each day. We remember with heartfelt gratitude those Crusaders who, in the prime of life, sacrificed 'their tomorrow for our today'.

21

FULL STEAM AHEAD

Back at Headquarters we on the staff were needing extra help. Dan Mahony had returned from Army Service in 1946 and in addition to handling the accounts he was re-establishing the Bookroom. Miss Amy Byrnell, Mr Vereker's excellent secretary who had continued loyally to support him throughout the war, was now working for me and proving a tower of strength – but the Union was getting into top gear and we were beginning to feel overwhelmed particularly where Camps and Houseparties were concerned.

The Camps Sub-Committee had as its Chairman one of the Union's most far sighted and discerning Leaders. Robert Ewan was a Chartered Accountant who, apart from organising a Christian Union at his old school, Christ's Hospital, devoted all his spare time to the Union in general and to Camps and Houseparties in particular. He persuaded his Sub-Committee to plan postwar camps on a scale that they, and I, at times felt to be almost reckless in size and scope. Would it be possible to find enough officers and staff to carry through the proposed programme? But his faith and zeal were gloriously vindicated. It was a thrilling time in so many ways, for although there were shortages of equipment and rationing of food, the joy of peace after six years of war produced a kind of happy abandon in the service of Christ – war certainly sorts out values and priorities.

In December 1947 our need for help at Headquarters was met in a most acceptable way when Donald Baker, a Crusader from Winchmore Hill Class, became my Assistant with particular responsibility for the Camps and Houseparties programme. Donald brought with him an eye for clarity of detail and a capacity for efficient planning, the like of which I had not come across before – nor have I since. We were a very happy team.

About this time we received some welcome help in the Bookroom from a Watford Crusader named Ray Bywaters who had just been demobilised from the Army. It was agreed he should stay with us for three months while he looked around for more permanent employment – in fact he remained with us for the rest of his working life, upwards of thirty years!

He was the exact opposite of Donald Baker, planning was not his line; like Pooh Bear, he was not an intellectual but he was pure gold. His quiet, simple deep love and devotion to Christ effused through all he said and did. Time would fail to tell how often we had to sort things out for him but, when we felt like showing him the door, his boyish guileless sincerity caused our hearts to overrule our heads!

No-one ever recruited boys to a Crusader Class in the way he did at Watford; he was a kind of Christian Pied Piper of Hamlyn; youngsters were attracted to him like metal to a magnet, but he just wanted them for Christ. His canoes on the local canal were among the many baits he used to catch boys, not by tens but, over the years, by hundreds. The Bishop of St Albans, himself an old Watford Crusader, was unable to attend Ray's funeral but instead wrote an appreciation which was read at the service; in it he referred warmly to 'dear old Ray' - it was a fitting epitaph.

By now things in the Union were quickly getting back to normal; mercifully in spite of the devastation all around St Paul's Cathedral, our offices at No 1 St Paul's Churchyard had escaped damage - there was not even a broken window. The 1946 Athletic Sports took place with over a thousand entries and, as mentioned before, a very ambitious camps programme was carried through successfully with more than a thousand boys involved.

Leaders were now being demobilised at a fast rate, and once they became acclimatised to civilian life again, not quite so easy as it may sound, they were keen to return to Crusader work. By March 1947 the number of Classes had risen to 233 with 11,434 on the roll: a year later there were 248 Classes with a membership of 13,325 - it was all very encouraging.

In those locations where numbers of Classes could be easily grouped, Area Committees were formed where Leaders could meet together at regular intervals to pray, plan and share experiences. This resulted in the introduction of local area events such as swimming galas, football and podex matches, rallies, competitions, sports days and, most important of all, consideration of ways and means of opening new Classes, and giving such new Classes practical help and support as they sought to get established.

Weekend residential Leaders' Conferences were now recommenced alternating between the North and South of England. One year at Swanwick in Derbyshire, the next at Hoddesdon in Hertfordshire; while Scotland and Ireland also had similar gatherings.

It would be hard to exaggerate the value of these occasions when Leaders could come apart to consider together ways and means of developing the work in their own Classes and in the Union at large, and prayerfully to make plans for the future. The warmth and loving regard each Leader had for the other is hard to describe satisfactorily; the sense of togetherness and of comradeship, the deep concern to glorify Christ, the personal heart-searching as gifted men of God opened up the Scriptures at devotional sessions, the serious desire to discover and to do the will of God in every aspect of daily life.

The memories of some older readers of these words will be stirred when mention is made of George and Montague Goodman, of Frank Bacon, John Stott, Alan Stibbs and there were many others – and in case the above comments paint too serious a picture, let it be said that it would be hard to find a group of men more ready with spontaneous humour and delighted laughter.

Leaders returned from these conferences with a deep sense of calling and of joyful heartfelt commitment to make their Classes 'the best for God'. There were no 'charismatics' in those days, no raising of arms, no drums or guitars, no hand clapping, no tongues, no words of knowledge, no offers of counselling. Could it be that these are 'signs of the times'? (Matt 16:3)

Whether Leaders were the poorer for the absence of these phenomena is an interesting question. However what is certain is that Crusader leadership meant wholehearted sacrifical service; boys taught from the Scriptures by means of carefully prepared talks, boys prayed for and cared for like a loving shepherd caring for his sheep, and boys brought by the Holy Spirit to true faith in Christ and then built up in Him with the result that, in the years that followed, hundreds left their Classes to serve God with the same determination which they had seen in their Leaders; many in so-called 'full-time' Christian work both at home and overseas.

During the war, and for quite a time afterwards, shortage of paper for printing was a problem, but gradually the situation eased and once again the magazine came into its own; soon the monthly circulation topped ten thousand and Cecil Allen, the honorary editor, continued to perform a great service in bringing the Union to the Union in a most acceptable and professional manner, and incidentally enabled hundreds of Associate Members to keep up-to-date with developments which, in turn, encouraged informed prayer support.

Most societies, Christian and otherwise, have a President chosen firstly because he approves the aims and methods of that particular society, and secondly because he is a recognised public figure and his name gives an assurance to the world at large that the movement, having his support, is a worthy one.

Often the appointment is rather a sinecure and this would be true of Lord Caldecote who was the Union's President for many years. He provided exactly what was required and occasionally acted as Chairman at Annual General Meetings in London. However when he died in 1947, the Commit-

General Sir Arthur Smith, President for 23 years

tee decided they would like a President who was more closely involved in the work of the Union and who better than Air Commodore P J Wiseman, CBE. He had been Commandant at countless Crusader camps and houseparties, had been Chairman of the General Committee, and had been the speaker at numerous Class Birthdays throughout the Union. His appointment in 1948 was warmly welcomed by Leaders but alas, he served in that capacity for only six months; his untimely death was a great loss to the movement.

When in due course it was announced that General Sir Arthur F Smith, KCB, KBE, DSO, MC, had accepted the Committee's invitation to become the next President, not many Leaders recognised the name or the significance of the appointment, but during the next twenty-three years they learnt what it meant to count on his help and support. He was willing to travel anywhere in order to serve as the Birthday speaker, and his simple, direct, straight from the shoulder talks always made a strong impression, as did his unusual humility. It was typical of the man that, in his later years, he decided to plan his own memorial service which he knew would inevitably take place in the Guards' Chapel in London.

It was a beautiful occasion with the Chapel Choir, the Band of the Guards plus the organ providing the music but it was glorifying only to Christ, not Arthur Smith. The Gospel was clearly proclaimed and so very typically, he succeeded in ensuring that his own name was mentioned once only during the whole of the service – he was like that. "My name's Smith, what's yours?" would be his opening remark on meeting a Crusader!

Having looked to the Air Force and the Army for their last two Presidents, the Committee decided that education should have a turn and who better to represent this increasingly important aspect of the Nation's life than Sir Eric Richardson, CBE, PhD, BEng, FIEE, who had recently retired from being Director of Education at the Regent Street Polytechnic, and who had previously been Principal of what is now known as the City University.

It was an excellent choice for once again here was a disciple of Christ who, like his predecessors, was willing to serve Crusaders without reserve, ably supported by May, his wife; a bonus indeed as together they acted as Host and Hostess at numerous Leaders' Conferences and other similar occasions over a period of fourteen years. When, in 1987, Sir Eric decided the time had come to retire, Rev Clive Calver was appointed in his place.

There have been many others who, over the years, have served the Union in an honorary capacity giving freely of their time and talents. Time would fail to tell of them all but some will remember John Farley who in the pre-war years helped at Headquarters dealing with the accounts, and who also made it financially possible for Captain Reginald Wallis to conduct a number of Class evangelistic campaigns over a period of six months.

John was followed by Newton Golden, a greatly respected Leader of several Classes, whose loving prayerful influence was an example and a blessing to all who knew him. It would be hard to exaggerate the value of the service rendered by John Miles who for many years handled, repaired and cared for all the Union's Camping Equipment which he kept in Birmingham. His practical inventiveness saved the camp account hundreds, if not thousands of pounds; incidentally enabling fees to be considerably less than would otherwise have been necessary. Others who helped at Headquarters in more recent years include Mrs Flora Sarpy, W J Taylor, Ken Devereux, Raymond Elgar, Harold Scott, Leslie Tucker and Dennis Lock. These are representative of a host of others who in one way and another have served the Union faithfully, joyfully and in most cases freely; motivated by gratitude for all Crusaders had meant to them in their early years when Christ first became a reality as Saviour, Lord and Friend.

Another aspect of Crusader activity which should not go unmentioned relates to School Christian Unions. They comprised Christian youngsters in their respective schools who met together, usually once a week in the dinner hour or after school, to encourage one another and to act as a witness to the significance of their faith. They often invited a visiting speaker to give a devotional talk. Frequently the boys leading these groups were Crusaders and Mr Vereker felt concerned to help them in their youthful and laudible responsibilites. Whatever he did must be unofficial for any outside influence would probably and quite reasonably be resented by the respective school authorities.

He managed to discover the names and addresses of many of the boys who were taking the lead and, once a year, he would invite as many as possible to tea in London during the school holidays. He used this opportunity, often with the co-operation of the Rev E J H Nash of the CSSM, to give advice, encouragement and guidance, the latter particularly in the realm where boyish zeal might step beyond the bounds of wisdom in the leadership of the CU.

Because many of these boys, in due course, went on to University, Dr Douglas Johnson, Secretary of the Inter-Varsity Fellowship was concerned to see them linked on to the Christian Unions in their respective locations. After the war it was therefore a very natural development for the CSSM, the IVF, the Girl Crusaders' Union and ourselves to get together with the aim of providing a more concerted help, and it was agreed to form the Inter-Schools Christian Fellowship (ISCF) under the auspices of a Committee comprising representatives from each of the four societies.

In the years that followed the work developed under the able guidance of Quintin Carr who, as mentioned previously, was a founder Leader of the Crusader Class in Glasgow and was later on the staff of the CSSM.

Travelling Secretaries were appointed who did a splendid work visiting school Christian Unions and helping new ones to form. Michael Hughes, an old Southgate Crusader, also on the staff of the CSSM produced a fine thought-provoking and spiritually stimulating magazine entitled 'The Pilgrim', particularly geared towards the more thoughtful schoolboy and schoolgirl. By 1949 no fewer than 72 school Christian Unions had become officially affiliated to the ISCF and a useful Fifth and Sixth Formers' Conference had taken place in London. However, the involvement of the four separate societies made for a somewhat unwieldy administration, and because all the staff and most of the finance was being provided by the CSSM it eventually, after several years, seemed sensible for that body to assume full control.

Early in 1948, a letter was received from the Council of the Girl Crusaders' Union inviting the boys' Union to join them in organising a Joint Autumn Bible School in London. It would be for Leaders, Assistant Leaders and seniors of sixteen and over. The proposal was warmly welcomed and Dr Graham Scroggie, a well known and much respected minister and preacher, accepted the invitation to be the lecturer; the venue chosen was St Peter's Church in Vere Street.

To everyone's delight the enterprise proved an outstanding success; at each of the sessions numbers were never less than four hundred, fairly equally divided between men and women and it was clear that a similar school must be held the following autumn. This duly took place with an enlarged pro- gramme; Dr Scroggie giving some of the lectures, while others were given by the Rev Alan Stibbs.

After several years and several different lecturers, numbers began to dwindle and in 1953 we joined with the Bible School at All Soul's Church, Langham Place under the Rev John Stott, the Rector. His contributions were outstanding and it was a great disappointment to many when this annual event came to an end. However in later years similar series of lectures were given by the Rev Dick Lucas of St Helen's Church, Bishopsgate.

About this time, certain members of the General Committee were approached by a number of Leaders of the Girl Crusaders' Union who were concerned at the introduction by their Council of a document entitled a 'Policy on Worldliness' which every Leader and Assistant Leader was requested to sign.

No-one doubted the genuine concern of the GCU Council to ensure a godly leadership but a significant number of their Leaders doubted the wisdom of seeking to secure it in this particular fashion and, in the course of time, the matter became an increasingly serious bone of contention.

The General Committee was informed of the upset but understandably did not feel they had any right, let alone desire, to interfere with the conduct of another organisation; on the other hand as a parallel organisation bearing the Crusader name they had reason to be concerned with the health and welfare of their sister movement. It was decided to inform the GCU Council of the reason for the Committee's interest and to ask if the Council would be willing to meet them in order to discuss the matter together. The GCU Council readily agreed and the meeting took place in March 1954; the subse- quent Committee minutes record that 'it had been as satisfactory as could be expected'. However in the months that followed no change in the Council's attitude was apparent, but it was learnt with relief that more than seventy

GCU Leaders had agreed to work together to try and persuade their Council to amend the policy.

To cut short a long and disappointing story, the dissident GCU Leaders, having failed in their endeavours, decided in 1955 that they could no longer remain in their Union; they would remove themselves and their Classes and form a separate new movement of their own, but expressed a strong preference to become an 'auxiliary' of the boys' Union. The reader can guess how much prayer, heart searching and discussion took place in the General Committee. They were not at all desirous of having the complication of a girls' movement on their hands; at the same time it seemed wholly undesirable for a completely new and separate girls' work to be formed, particularly when the dissident lady leaders were Crusaders for whose cause the Committee had every sympathy. It also meant explaining the situation to all elected boys' Leaders and the holding of a Special Business Meeting to secure approval or otherwise for any proposed action, and the alteration of the Union's Constitution.

Endeavour after endeavour was made to try and find a way of healing the situation and restoring harmony in the GCU but without avail. Eventually on 18th October 1955 the General Committee decided 'that the necessary preparatory steps be taken to lead to the formation of a Girls' Auxiliary with a view to such an organisation coming into being on 1st January 1956, unless in the meantime some circumstance arises which affords reasonable grounds for believing that the breach within the Girl Crusaders' Union will be healed'.

So it was that on 1st January 1956 the Crusaders' Union Girls' Association (not Auxiliary) came into being. Mrs Barbara Atkins, Leader of the Whetstone Class, became the Honorary Secretary and a room in her house was made available as an office. They would elect their own Committee and their decisions would be 'subject to the General Committee'.

Every member of the General Committee earnestly hoped that this would soon turn out to be a temporary measure, but by 17th February 1956, fourteen Girls' Classes and their Leaders had applied for affiliation. In the weeks and months that followed the number steadily grew and to everyone's disappointment the possibility of a reconciliation became less and less likely. In due course a CUGA badge was produced similar to the boys' badge except that the top of the shield was scalloped.

In the years that followed the Girls' Association continued on its separate way, organising its own Conferences, Houseparties, Rallies, Sports Days, Prayer Meetings, Magazine and the weekly Returns Sheet, with the Boys'

Headquarters lending a helpful hand whenever needed. A Minute of the General Committee dated 21st January 1958 records the following:

'The CUGA Committee had sent a gift of £35 as a token of appreciation of the help given in various ways by Headquarters.'

There were now more than seventy Classes in the Association and their Committee decided the time had come to acquire a Headquarters in central London and to appoint a full-time Secretary. During her four years as Hon Secretary, Mrs Atkins had made a tremendous contribution in establishing the administration on a firm and efficient footing but she too was concerned to see a more permanent arrangement.

It was agreed that they should locate their office as near as possible to the Union Headquarters so that their Leaders could visit and use the Bookroom. Eventually two rooms became available on the first floor of No 29 Ludgate Hill and although not particularly attractive, it was decided to take these in the hope that in due course accommodation might become available up the Hill at No 1 – the building occupied by the Union.

No doubt the world would call it coincidence (but Christians know better) when at this time a lady named Miss Mary Bevington was prayerfully considering her future. Yes, she was none other than the daughter of Herbert Bevington who had played so large a part in establishing and developing the boys' Union.

Mary had joined the Finchley Girls' Class when nine years old and later had become an Assistant Leader there until she joined the WAAF in World War II. After the War she became a member of the staff of the Church Pastoral Aid Society from which she had retired six months previously after serving there for some twelve years, during which time she had been involved in their youth work.

It did not take the CUGA Committee long to decide that here was exactly the help they needed and Mary was invited to become their first paid Secretary with effect from 1st January 1960, working initially for three days each week.

From the earliest days of the Association, Houseparties and Camps had been introduced and these had been steadily developed under the guidance of Mrs Flora Sarpy, a Leader of the Wandsworth Common Class. For some time she had also been working at Union headquarters in connection with the Forces scheme, which involved maintaining contact with Cruaders doing their National Service, however with the move to No 29 Ludgate Hill completed, it was thought that the girls' Camps work should also be handled from there and so Mrs Sarpy, as their part-time Camps Secretary, was seconded for

Officers at the first CUGA Houseparty in 1957

Barbara Atkins, Honorary Secretary of the CUGA, 1956-1960

Mary Bevington, General Secretary of the CUGA, 1960-1975

one day each week to work at No 29, ably helped by Mrs Marjorie Wakely, also much involved with camps. When after some four years, pressure of other duties forced Mrs Sarpy to reliquish her position, Mrs Wakely became the next Camps' Secretary.

By now the Association had a full programme of those events and happenings which one would expect to find in a virile youth movement; net-ball rallies, tennis rallies, athletic sports, campers' re-unions, conferences for Leaders and Assistant Leaders, rallies in London and a rally in Manchester, the production of a magazine and last, but certainly not least, regular meetings for prayer. In every way it was a time of great encouragement and joyful enthusiasm.

In 1960 the ladies were invited to join the men at their bi-annual conference for Leaders at Swanwick and 42 Girls' Classes were represented by 72 Leaders. A year later the first mixed houseparty for senior boys' and girls' took place at Clarens in Switzerland, shortly followed by a similar houseparty at Bonskeid House near Pitlochry in Scotland, and a joint climbing venture based at Keswick. Gradually the two movements were beginning to grow together.

The steady growth of the girls' work was such that office space at 29 Ludgate Hill was becoming a problem, so too was the disadvantage of not being in the same building as the boys. At long last accommodation became available on the 5th floor of No 1 and the Spring of 1963 saw the ladies happily established there, with No 29 satisfactorily sub-let to the Girl Covenanters' Union.

It is interesting to look back now and to recognise how what initially had seemed unthinkable was beginning to take place. On 17th November 1964 a supper was planned for the boys' and girls' Committees to be followed by a general discussion and the Minutes record:

'As the discussion developed members became increasingly impressed with the importance of ensuring greater co-operation, and a certain amount of integration between the boys' and girls' sides of the work.' With the intro-duction of comprehensive education and the gradual disappearance of many single sex schools, it could only be a matter of time before the arrival of mixed Crusader Classes in some places, all the more so because not infrequently the Leaders of the Girls' Classes in a particular location were none other than the wives of the men leading the Boys' Classes!

Whether they were Leaders or no, the wives of Crusader Leaders often played a very significant part behind the scenes in supporting their husbands, providing the food for Birthday Squashes or laying on an attractive spread when, after Class on Sundays, their husbands brought boys home to tea. This was an excellent means for Leaders to get to know their members better and incidentally, for some boys, it was their first experience of a truly Christian home.

Having in mind their valued ministry, it was decided to plan a weekend conference specially for Leaders and their wives. A Methodist Holiday Home called 'The Links' at Eastbourne was secured and the weekend proved so popular that similar conferences were held annually for many years. Some reading these lines will recall with pleasure and gratitude the ministry of the Rev F Kerr-Dineen, the local Rector of Holy Trinity Church, who frequently gave the devotional talks which were among the most helpful some of us had ever heard.

During all this time the boys' work continued to make encouraging progress; new Classes were being elected at an average of one per month and each year unusual and exciting events such as gliding, go-cart racing and other challenging ventures were being added to the camping and holiday pro-gramme. In addition our island centre at Westbrook was playing an increasingly valuable part in the Crusader work, there each summer holiday saw five consecutive canvas camps of a hundred boys each in the spacious grounds under semi-luxurious conditions, for the house could be used for meals and, on those few occasions when a camper was unwell, he could be put to bed in one of the rooms.

Gradually additional facilities were added to Westbrook; first the enlarge-ment of the dining room, then the addition of two more dormitories plus an officers' room. After that a sizeable games hall, invaluable in wet weather, followed by a hobbies hut equipped with two lathes and much else besides. Later with assistance from the Navy at Portsmouth an assault course was erected and another very popular addition was a 9-hole pitch-and-putt golf course.

In 1954 A J Vereker, after seven years as Warden, decided the time had come to retire. It would be hard to over-estimate all he had meant to the Union. Under him the movement had become firmly established and vigorously developed and now the same was true of Westbrook.

He had come to love the Isle of Wight where life was, and perhaps still is, lived at a somewhat more leisurely pace and, having found a small but attrac-tive property at Binsteed with a garden bordering on a golf club, he and Mrs Vereker together with their two daughters were soon happily established there and, typical of the man, it was only a matter of months before he became the golf club's secretary! Sadly he was killed some years later driving his car in the very early morning when, rounding a bend, he suddenly met a milk lorry coming in the opposite direction on the wrong side of the road. It could be said with all fairness that the Union is his memorial.

Earlier when A J Vereker had announced his intention to retire, Ivan Gowing-Scopes and his wife were attracted to the possibility that perhaps they might take over the work at Westbrook. For several years Ivan had been Leader of the flourishing Orpington and Hatch End classes, and, having a strong artistic bent plus considerable experience in printing, he had been a valued advisor when guidance was needed at Union Headquarters in connection with printed material such as annual reports, motto cards, holiday brochures and the like.

He was an excellent successor ideally suited to continue and develop what A J Vereker had begun and, over the next eighteen years, Ivan and Joan became much loved and respected for the friendly and warm-hearted way they served and co-operated with the hundreds of Crusaders, and others, who made use of Westbrook.

Now in addition to camps, Westbrook provided an attractive venue for conferences and Leadership Training weekends, and individual Classes and groups of Classes were able to organise houseparties for their members; it also became a popular place for 'school journeys' at those times when it was not required for Crusaders, which helped to make Westbrook financially self-supporting.

Today Westbrook is more valuable to Crusaders than it has ever been. From 1984 to 1992 Peter White, a former Sheffield Leader, was the Manager and he and his wife, Sheila, gave themselves unstintingly to the Centre and expanded its work considerably. The Headingley Lounge, the Orchard Camp, the sub-division of most of the large rooms in to more manageable units and a fine heated swimming pool were some of the many additions and improvements while Peter and Sheila were at the Centre. The pool was generously donated by Sir Maurice Laing, whose father did so much for Westbrook in earlier days.

The present Manager is Stephen Foster and he and his wife, Catriona, have very quickly shown themselves to be the ideal couple to run the Centre and continue its ministry to so many in Crusaders and from churches and schools.

Ivan and Joan Gowing-Scopes, Wardens at Westbrook for 18 years

*Crusader Headquarters
at 1 Ludgate Hill*

*The Bookroom –
a part of the
Headquarters*

22

CO-OPERATION INDEED

No history of Crusaders would be complete without reference to the way it was possible for the Headquarters to remain in so suitable and central a location as Ludgate Hill. In the early 1950's our lease came to an end and we waited somewhat anxiously to hear from the landlord's agent, for any new offer might well be beyond our financial ability.

After some months we discovered that consideration was being given by the City Corporation to a 'St Paul's Precinct Plan'. The area to the north and north west of St Paul's had been devastated by German bombs – it was amazing that the Cathedral had suffered so little damage and now it was a question of how to re-develop the whole site. We learnt that consideration was being given to the idea of demolishing all the remaining buildings around St Paul's Churchyard to make way for a grand new arrangement with St Paul's at the centre. Should this be decided on, then our building would be included in the demolition.

The cost of so grandiose a project would have been enormous, for the owners of the many large buildings, like ours, would have had to be compensated. So the months and years went by and during this period of indecision, no question of a new lease was put to us and we just went on paying the same very reasonable rent.

Some years before this and unknown to us, the ownership of our building had changed hands; it had been bought by the Co-operative Insurance Society (CIS) of Manchester. Eventually towards the end of 1956, the City authorities decided not to touch the buildings on our side of the Cathedral and soon after I had a phone call from our owner's agents. My heart sank as I feared the worst, no doubt we would now have to look for offices we could afford.

"You realise, don't you," began the gentleman on the other end of the line, "that your lease expired some time ago, it's not very satisfactory is it?" "Well," I replied, "it suits us very well!" He laughed, "I'm sure it does, having in mind the rent you are now paying." My heart sank still further, then he said, "I've received instructions from the owners, the like of which I have never had in all my years as an estate agent." I wondered what was coming as he went on, "We've been told to deal generously with you!" My heart leapt with joy as he continued: "Well, what do you think?"

It seemed like Nehemiah all over again when the King of Babylon enquired of him, "For what do you make request? So I prayed to the God of heaven and I said..." I too momentarily lifted up my heart to God as I referred to the rent we had been paying and, almost without thinking, suggested a very modest increase to £605 per annum. He hesitated for a moment and then said: "All right, in a situation like this your guess is as good as mine."

Not only was it £605 per annum inclusive, but it was for 21 years with the right on our side to end the agreement at 7 and at 14 years if we so wished. How we thanked God, for not only was this an answer to our prayers, it was, as with Nehemiah, a clear sign of the good hand of our God upon us and upon what we were seeking to do, and a joyful spur to further endeavour. Now whenever I walk across Paternoster Square, which in due course arose out of the devastation to the North of St Paul's, I recall with grateful thanks those exciting days of post-war Britain. I gather from recent comments in the press that the powers that be now dislike, and would like to change, what the architects and planners eventually did with that derelict bomb site where once I, and many others, parked our cars.

Incidentally we never discovered the human element involved in our new lease, but it is clear someone in authority in the CIS knew about and approved of the work being done by Crusaders and had instructed the agents to deal generously with us - it was a wonderfully kind gesture. We now had every reason to put in hand the complete re-planning and re-equipping of our offices and bookroom and this was done with the help and co-operation of a Crusader named Douglas Thornton, a wartime pilot in the RAF who later became a missionary with the Africa Inland Mission, but who had to return home suddenly on the death of his father, to take charge of the family building firm of Ashby and Horner in London. Thanks to him and his firm's expertise, we soon had a Bookroom second to none in style and modernity.

Nor was this all the story where No 1 Ludgate Hill (or No 1 St Paul's Churchyard, both are correct!) is concerned for, many years later when the remainder of the building had become occupied by a fast developing firm called the Abbey Life Assurance Co Ltd, there came a time when they urgently needed the whole of the floor, on part of which our Headquarters was located. After financial inducements failed, they finally offered us an increased area on another floor and agreed to re-establish us there free of charge. This was an offer too good to miss for it enabled the Girls' Associa-

The General Committee in 1956

Left to right: Back row – Michael Thomas, Jim Stunt, Lewis Fletcher, John Miles, John Redfern, Douglas Combridge, Bill Burkett
Middle row – Bill Chapman, Derek Warren, David Thompson, Harry Green, Randle Manwaring, Kenneth Anderson, Dick Trew, Jack Watford
Front row – Roy Cattell, Alan Brown, Montague Goodman, Frank Bacon, John Laing, Herbert Bevington, Alan Farrin, Bill Sharpe, Robert Ewan

tion to join us, and so we became one first-rate Headquarters and Bookroom, ideal for all our needs and at no extra cost to ourselves.

The story of these events is quickly told, but of course it involved much prayer and thought, much careful negotiation, detailed planning and legal agreements, and finally a period of chaos as the re-arrangements were put in hand; but when at last it was all over we had every reason yet again to 'raise our Ebenezer' and proclaim with glad thanksgiving 'hitherto has the Lord helped us'.

The foundation of the Crusaders' Union was, without any doubt, the quality of its Leaders; during my forty years at HQ it was my privilege to visit Class after Class for Birthday weekends and similar happy events and I invariably returned home filled with admiration for, and appreciation of, all I had seen and heard. Were I to choose one word to describe those Leaders, the one most appropriate would be devotion.

First and foremost a personal devotion to Christ and all that this comprised in the practical and sensible outworking of their spiritual lives. Allied to this was their devotion to and familiarity with the Scriptures, and I mean all the Scriptures; the relevance of the Old Testament and the significance of the New. Finally, it was their devotion to the boys in their Classes which was the inevitable corollary of their love for the living and the written Word.

It was from this galaxy of discipleship that the General Committee was elected each year and from which the various Sub-Committees were appointed. The heart of the Union's administration was a small group appointed by the General Committee which met over a sandwich lunch, every Thursday from 1-2 pm. It was called the General Purposes Sub-Committee composed of Leaders, mostly working in central London, who were at the top of their professions or vocations and so in a position to leave their places of work for a short time each week.

Chairman of this Sub-Committee for 37 years was Frank D Bacon whose loving, warm-hearted, perceptive nature enriched all who knew him. It would be hard to over-estimate his influence on the Union's work. Having mentioned Frank Bacon, I went on to recall and began to describe others who served with him during those years, but as memory got to work I found myself confronted with more than two dozen names, all of whom deserved to be extolled, together with many others. Finally reluctantly and unwillingly I was forced to accept the fact that my descriptions would mean very little to the majority of those reading these lines. I hope and believe none will be offended by the decision to omit the appreciations I would gladly have included. Happily enough they are all known to the One to whom, in the first instance, they gave their service.

Week by week over the years these men considered every facet of the Union's work so that each month, the General Committee had presented to them, reports, recommendations and suggestions which had already been carefully examined and sifted – not for rubber stamping but so that the members, from all four corners of the movement, could examine and discuss proposals from the standpoint of the areas they represented and incidentally in doing so, avoided the possibility of a London based outlook.

To be with these men and to hear their discussion was an inspiration in itself; differing views would be expressed with clarity and conviction, but gradually there would come a sense of direction. The guidance of God had been sought at the start of the meeting and the Holy Spirit was gently showing the way to a final happy agreement. Clearly an example of 'those who by reason of use have their senses exercised to discern' Hebrews 5:14. It was a heart-warming experience for me as, in many ways, I was living a sheltered life surrounded by Christians, while they were in the hard outside world and so were better able to apply up-to-date ideas to the ever-changing conditions of contemporary life.

The year 1956 was a time of thanksgiving for it saw the celebration of the Union's Golden Jubilee which included an inspiring and heart-warming Conference of Leaders at Swanwick; the publication of a booklet entitled: 'These Fifty Years' which presented a brief history of the movement and, most dramatic of all, two Rallies in the Royal Albert Hall.

The afternoon Rally was mainly for Classes from the provinces and the programme was repeated in the evening for the Classes in and around London. The hall was full on both occasions which meant that more than twelve thousand Crusaders had participated.

We believe we made a bit of history on that occasion for we wanted to include a Union film as part of the programme but were confidently informed by the authorities at the hall that, while it was possible to project a commercial sized film, the throw from the Royal Box to the screen was far too great for our small 16 mm Kodachrome film. However we discovered that a certain projection firm had just acquired a new projector which had a greatly increased light source, and they readily agreed to test the possibility of doing what had not been done previously in the Albert Hall. To our great delight, and that of the firm, the experiment was a complete success, and a half-hour film of the Union's activities was included in the programme. We were subsequently very gratified to receive from Leaders, many letters of appreciation, their members had been very impressed to see the Union in so large a situation, and had much enjoyed all that had been provided for them which had included visits to interesting places in London. It was a day to remember!

I couldn't really blame the London Bible College in 1957 for seeing in Donald Baker just the man they were needing to be their Secretary, but I was very sad to lose him. We had worked happily together for almost ten years and during that time we had received much encouragement in all sections of the work. However help was close at hand for a few months earlier the Committee had given me an assistant in the person of Michael Freegard, whose father had been my much loved Leader when I was a boy and later, a co-leader in the Muswell Hill Class. I had known Michael from birth and when he joined the HQ staff it did not take long to discover in him, a young man of considerable ability.

He happily took on Donald Baker's job of Camps Secretary and later, in addition, became Editor of an inset of 'The Crusaders' Magazine' entitled 'The Junior Crusader', serving the younger members of the Union.

Michael had a questioning, probing mind and was quick to see and suggest possibilities for improvement in the administration. His fellowship and loyal support meant a great deal to me during the eight years we were together, but then he had the unique opportunity to join and become ultimately responsible for the Performing Rights Society, and so I lost another much appreciated colleague.

As mentioned previously, many Crusaders heard and responded to the call of the overseas mission field, and notwithstanding the closure of China where upwards of forty Crusaders had been working, there were in 1956 one hundred and eighty in other parts of the world. We were concerned to retain as close a link as possible with these men and they were all sent a Crusader Magazine each month and, in addition, from time to time each received a personal letter from Herbert Pateman who for 21 years was our Honorary Missionary Secretary. He was also Leader of the Leicester East Class and incidentally the father of the Rev Norman Pateman who, after service in China, became Secretary of the China Inland Mission, later renamed the Overseas Missionary Fellowship. For a number of years Norman was Chairman of our Camps Sub-Committee and served regularly as Padre at summer camps.

23

THE DIAMOND JUBILEE

It was in March 1964 that our thoughts first began to turn to the importance of 1966; it would see the Union's Diamond Jubilee, how could we best recognise and celebrate this significant anniversary? Like Queen Victoria of old, we too would look back on 'sixty glorious years' during which, in a quite remarkable way, God had blessed and used this somewhat anomalous movement: anomalous because although all its Leaders were faithful church members, it had functioned like a missionary society, outside the aegis of the various denominations; incidentally an excellent example of virile ecumenicism, although few at the time would have recognised the word, let alone understood what it meant!

Of course there was always the Royal Albert Hall where previous important anniversaries had been celebrated, but the Committee felt that this time the character of the occasion seemed to call more for heartfelt thanksgiving rather than for an exciting meeting which had, quite properly, characterised previous rallies.

My office windows looked out over the Dean of St Paul's garden and sometimes I could hear piano music coming from one of the rooms below. What about a great Service of Thanksgiving in St Paul's Cathedral? The idea appealed to the Committee, we could at least make enquiries.

I climbed the well-worn steps and knocked on the door of the ancient Deanery which had escaped both the fire of London and the German bombs; yes, Dr Matthews was expecting me, and as I walked across the entrance hall, the uneven surface of the polished wood floor gave further evidence to the antiquity of the place. My subsequent record of that interview states:

'The Dean was friendly and favourable but permission had to be obtained from the Chapter. There would need to be a printed and approved programme, the organist would have to be paid a fee whether he played or not; if anyone other than an Anglican clergyman were to give the address, the Bishop's permission would be needed.'

Dr Matthews finally referred me to a Mr Floyd Ewin who was Registrar and Receiver of St Paul's, whose kind, courteous helpfulness at a subsequent meeting was greatly appreciated. From him I learned that the cost of hiring the Cathedral was £150 which included the services of the choir and vergers. We could save £40 by dispensing with the choir but past experience had taught that would be most inadvisable. With chairs in the side aisles the Cathedral could accommodate 3,800 persons.

The General Committee was unanimous in deciding that this was a most appropriate and acceptable way to celebrate the Union's Jubilee and in the months that followed we made our plans. It proved to be a most memorable occasion. The service was led by Canon Geoffrey Rogers of Lee Abbey fame who, in earlier days had been a Leader of the Cambridge Class, and the address was given by the Rev John Stott, then Rector of All Soul's Church, Langham Place, and a much loved Vice-President of the Union.

The Cathedral was full to overflowing; the organ was in the hands of the Deputy organist and, to our joy, we discovered he had been a Crusader as a boy and knew exactly how to lead Crusader singing. I could not help laughing to myself as I watched the faces of the choir; after the first verse of the first hymn they smiled at each other as they realised there was no question of them giving a lead. I really think they enjoyed having a congregation that knew how to sing, the praise came from our hearts as well as our voices – we could have saved that £40! Incidentally the Dean asked to read one of the lessons, it was a kindly gesture, perhaps he remembered the time in his boyhood when he was a member of the Scripture Union. Close by the Cathedral is the delightful hall of the Stationers' Company and they generously put it at our disposal so that, after the Service, we were able to provide tea for the VIPs, appropriately welcomed and received by Sir Arthur and Lady Smith.

But this was not all, the Committee felt the year of Jubilee should be marked by a financial appeal, and an attractive brochure had been prepared and circulated, it contained an interesting proposition. For some time Leaders in the Midlands and the North had felt somewhat envious of the southern Classes for whom Westbrook on the Isle of Wight was convenient and easily reached; northerners were not so well placed, what about another Crusader Centre more easily accessible for them? The Committee had every sympathy with the idea and the Jubilee Appeal brochure gave, as the main aim, the provision of such a place. The collection taken at the Service of Thanksgiving gave the Appeal Fund a healthy start and the search began for 'The Crusader Centre of the North'.

The Leaders in the Midlands, Merseyside and Manchester Areas lost no time in seeking a suitable place and soon Ken Johnston, a Leader of the Manchester Heaton Moor Class and a member of the General Committee,

St Paul's Cathedral – a fitting place for Thanksgiving

Cae Canol, Beddgelert – a perfect location in Snowdonia

was presenting a report compiled by Norman Elston, a Leader of Manchester Hale Class, telling of a place called 'Tower Wood' located on the Northern shores of Lake Windermere. It sounded an attractive proposition and so we made arrangements to see the property and found a well-maintained, well-sited mansion looking out across the lake. There was a large stone-built boathouse, not in the sale, which would prove a useful asset if available. The house could accommodate at least forty in fair-sized rooms, unfortunately the grounds were rough and uneven and unsuitable for normal camping. To cut a long story short, having decided to purchase the place we found ourselves 'gazumped' and the deal fell through.

During the subsequent months the search continued, but for some time nothing really suitable was found until one day someone noticed an advertisement telling of a farmhouse for sale just outside Beddgelert in North Wales; those who went to see it were thrilled with its possibilities for the property looked directly across open country to Snowdon and the Welsh mountain range. Although somewhat smaller than 'Tower Wood', the price was considerably less so there would be money available for its adaptation and enlargement.

So it was that before long, Ken Johnston, Norman Elston and I were sitting in the lounge of that farmhouse discussing the matter with the friendly farmer and his wife; she had arthritis and they wanted to move to a bungalow they owned down the lane. We soon felt convinced that this was the answer to our many prayers - the place was right, the price was right, and now, all we needed was official approval for a 'change of use' from farmhouse to youth centre.

We decided to go on at once to Caernarvon to secure the necessary permission and then the purchase could be finalised without any further delay. We located the Council offices and were shown into the room of the official concerned with such matters. He greeted us courteously and asked what we wanted. We explained our mission - yes, he knew the area well and yes, he knew the farmhouse too, what did we want it for? "A Youth Centre?" he smiled, "I'm afraid you haven't a hope," he said. We looked puzzled and asked why permission should be withheld.

"Do you realise," he said, "You're talking about Snowdon National Park; it's a very carefully controlled area. There are already a considerable number of youth and similar centres and, like you, many more would like to come. I am Secretary of the Committee responsible for the area and its members decided, quite a long time ago, that no more youth centres should be allowed. I'm sorry but you are wasting your time, there's no point in your putting in an application."

This was the last thing we had expected, it was a shattering blow. We had felt so sure that we had experienced the guidance of God in a strangely certain way - had we deceived ourselves? After a pause I said, "Can you give us any advice?", hoping that there might yet be some way round the problem. "Why yes," he said, "there are two things you could do, one is find a Youth Centre already in existence which is wanting to pull out, purchase it and you can then take over the right to remain a Youth Centre, but I'm afraid you won't find one - once in, they stay. The second thing you can do is find a place outside Snowdon National Park, say down in the Cader Idris area and you'll have no problem."

We felt very crestfallen; it meant we were back to square one. It was a case of Nehemiah all over again. I lifted up my heart in a quick desperate prayer and without rhyme or reason I said, "You're not Welsh are you?" "No, I'm English" he replied. Still enquiring I said, "What brought you to Wales?" He smiled, "I married a Welsh girl during the war." "Where did the war take you?" I asked. He laughed, "No one has ever heard of the place where I fetched up." "Where was that?", I enquired. "A place in the Far East called Cox's Bazar." Now it was my turn to smile, "I know Cox's Bazar" I said. He looked amazed, "You know Cox's Bazar?" "Yes", I said. "During the war I was an Explosives Officer in the RAF and for a time I was Commanding Officer of a main Explosives Unit in Chittagong with responsibility for Sub-Units down the Arakan coast of Burma at Akyab, Ramree, Ultakhali and one at Cox's Bazar!"

"Do you know," he said, "You're the first person I've met since the war ended who had even heard of Cox's Bazar." He was obviously delighted and for quite a time we talked about our experiences in the Far East generally and at Cox's Bazar in particular. Suddenly he broke off, "You know old friend, there's no reason why you shouldn't put in an application for a change of use at that farm, in fact I'll do it for you." Out came a plan of the locality which he photo-copied for us and soon I was putting my signature to the Application Form! Inside I was bursting with gratitude to God. We shook hands and departed after expressing our appreciation, knowing for certain like Isaac's servant of old, "I being in the way, the Lord led me..." Gen 24:27 AV. A few weeks later we received the permission for 'change of use'!

The name of the farmhouse is Cae Canol and all down the years it has been a place of blessing to countless Crusaders. Thanks to the devotion of Norman Elston and his wife, and many willing volunteers, it has not been necessary to have a resident warden and so the fees charged have gone towards all kinds of fine improvements which have made it a perfect centre in an idyllic setting. I understand Cae Canol is Welsh for 'Middle Field'; recalling that interview in Caernarvon I sometimes think we could quite justifiably have changed the name to Cox's Bazar!

As I look back over the years, memory recalls face after face of the dozens of young men and women who, for various lengths of time, were my colleagues at Headquarters. We could not have got by without their willing, warm-hearted, efficient support. Each replacement fitted happily into the team and, in a detailed history, each would merit a mention; I hope they will forgive me if they have looked in vain for their names to be included, their omission in no way indicates any lack of appreciation on my part.

There were of course, some whose particular responsibilities call for specific mention and two such joined the staff in the autumn of 1965. Tony Goodwin from the Birmingham Erdington Class took over as Camps Administrator, and Peter Finnie of Leicester Knighton Class became my assistant. Peter had just completed four years as Travelling Secretary for the Training Colleges' Christian Fellowship - a branch of the Inter-Varsity Fellowship, and had intended to return to the Textile Industry, when he heard of our need and responded to it.

His appointment meant a great deal to me for, not only did he share in the ever-increasing work-load, but his quiet warm-hearted nature made him a very easy colleague with whom to integrate, as together we dealt with the many facets of our Headquarters activities.

Peter loved camping and was much in demand to act as Padre at Class, Area and Union Camps. He was also a very acceptable speaker at Class Birthdays and similar functions even though in some ways he was rather a 'loner' and loved going for long walks by himself; he was also a very strong swimmer.

His many Union commitments did not prevent him being a much loved Leader of the Cockfosters Class; he believed it was important to retain a positive link with the grass roots of the movement and once remarked, "It is not easy to belong everywhere and at the same time nowhere" a typical example of his sensible outlook.

Alas, Peter's involvement in the Union ended in the saddest possible way. In 1972 Trevor Jones, a leader of the Lancing Class, retired early from his job as a Heating Engineer, to become Assistant Warden of Westbrook and he and Olive, his wife, moved into the gardener's cottage on the estate. Their highly practical and deeply spiritual support meant a great deal to the Warden who at the time was Graham Sturton. Graham had returned from missionary service with the Sudan United Mission and previously had been a member of the Gloucester Class.

In the summer of 1976 a pair of new canoes had been acquired for Westbrook and Peter Finnie was keen to try them out, so too was Trevor and they agreed a date when this would be possible. On the day in question they took the canoes down to the beach below Westbrook and set out from there in weather conditions which appeared perfectly reasonable, they were experienced canoeists and both were wearing life-jackets.

There are times in life when the eye of faith must look at human happenings through tears of grief, for Peter and Trevor failed to return. Trevor's body was found the next day near Ryde pier: it was several days before Peter's was found near the mainland. We shall never know in this life how it was that two men of such experience on water should have come to grief in a pair of brand new canoes. Apart from the war years, this was the greatest tragedy suffered by the Union in all its history. The extent to which we missed these two fine men of God was the measure of our deep appreciation of them.

It was typical of Randle Manwaring, a member of the General Committee, to take his gifted pen and compose, in memoriam, a poem entitled 'Two Canoes' which was printed in the Autumn number of 'Crusader Review'. Part of that poem reads as follows:

'Their aims that day, as ever, were the highest,
The greatest good of those within their care;
The tests they made were for the benefit
Of those whose joys they came to prepare.

For this their lives were lived until that hour
For the blessing of the world Christ came to save;
This was the constant aim of both always
And in this spirit met the wind and wave.

How like the sea on which we sail, the storms,
The short-lived perils, buffeting us all
In little ships. These two knew One who gave
Himself to reach us in life's rise and fall.

And as we mourn the loss of two who lived
Within the limits of foreshortened days,
We know their struggle with the sea completed
Glad offerings of service and of praise.'

24

STRATEGY FOR THE SEVENTIES

With the arrival of the year 1970, someone on Committee coined the phrase: 'Strategy for the Seventies' as it was realised that before the decade had run its course, many basic decisions would have to be made. Among the most important of these was the question of the future location of Headquarters for, although our lease did not terminate until Christmas 1977, it was most unlikely we would be granted a new one and certainly not at a rent we could afford. Accordingly an 'Accommodation Working Party' was appointed and time would fail to tell of the number of possibilities considered in the months and years that followed.

It seemed desirable to remain in central London, not only because many Leaders worked there and so could visit the Bookroom and serve on Committees and Working parties, but also because so many leaders visited London from all over the country from time to time, and many made a point of coming in for a chat. This facility was most valuable, concerned as we were to try and ensure no leader felt remote from the centre, and could drop in at any time and be warmly welcomed.

I valued such visits enormously for it enabled me to forge and sustain personal links with each leader, to share in his encouragements and hopes for the future and to learn of the problems and challenges he was facing. This often led on quite naturally to a short time of prayer together as we remembered the particular needs of his Class. I like to think that most went on their way refreshed and encouraged, certainly their warm fellowship meant much to me. I well recall receiving a letter from a leader of a provincial Class shortly after he had visited Headquarters, he wrote:

'It remains something of a mystery why I have never been before. After feeling remote and rather isolated (not your fault, but mine) I really felt I belonged. So the irritations I had passed over were opportunities missed. So be it. That's past. The future beckons. And I return to God's work heartened and renewed in an unexpected way.'

So we persevered in our searching for a new Headquarters and prayed for guidance. The London City Mission was seeking permission to build a new headquarters on the site of a disused church near the southern end of Tower Bridge, they indicated they might have spare accommodation to rent but, in our heart of hearts, we hoped for a place of our own. Then we heard of a property near London Bridge available for purchase for £80,000 but it would need at least another £50,000 to convert to office use; members of Committee who visited the place were not impressed.

Consideration was given to an idea that we might perhaps link up with several other like-minded societies thus providing a kind of united Christian Centre, but this possibility was soon dropped. Another idea was to build our own Headquarters in the lovely grounds of Oak Hill Theological College in Southgate. The Trustees of the College were not unfavourable to the suggestion and the General Committee minutes of October 1972 indicate they were: 'making tentative enquiries of the Planning Authorities as to whether there would be a possibility of erecting an office block somewhere in the College grounds'.

I cannot recall what the local authority said but the matter was not proceeded with.

Each month the item 'HQ Accommodation' appeared on the General Committee agenda and, with it, a reminder that time was passing all too quickly. Suddenly in the Autumn of 1973 it seemed that our needs could be met in Chiswick.

The Crusader Class there had its own most attractive purpose-built hall which at one time had been the centre of much Crusader activity but, over the years, the area had changed and now numbers were very small and the outlook bleak. The Crusader Trustees of the hall willingly co-operated with the suggestion that the premises be adapted as Union Headquarters and our Crusader architect, Eric Starling, prepared an excellent outline plan which he submitted to the local Authority. During the months that followed all kinds of complications were raised and fresh plans were submitted and, to cut a long and tedious story short, the proposal was finally abandoned and, once again, we were back to square one.

In July 1974 the record states that Michael Penny, a leader of the Southgate Class and a member of the General Committee reported that 'the Accommodation Working Party had looked at a number of properties but so far there had been no further developments. They were still thinking in terms of a property within a 30-35 mile radius of London in the North or Northwest area.'

So it was that in September 1974, St Albans was mentioned for the first time and members of Committee began to realise that if London had to be left behind, then St Albans had much to commend it. It was close to the M1 and so easily reached from the Midlands and the North and, in addition, there was news of plans for another motorway, the M25, which would completely circumnavigate London in the form of a ringway, which would also have to pass fairly close to St Albans; clearly the place would become an important and easily reached centre.

By March 1975 a disused school in the city had been considered, also a redundant church but neither really commended themselves, but in April it was learnt that the St Albans Abbey authorities had put their Abbey Institute on the market, and some of us went to see it. Apart from a room containing library books it was internally a very unattractive place, it had an uncared for look and made one think of Victoriana and Dickens! But the building itself was sound and if the inside were completely gutted, redesigned and modernised, it could clearly provide all we required and more; in addition its location in the shadow of the Abbey was perfect.

Adjoining the Institute was a place called Tankerfield House which was divided into two flats occupied by Abbey Vergers, that too was in the sale.

The General Committee Minutes of May 1975 contain the following:

'A memorandum from Mr Michael Penny was tabled in which he put forward his reason for recommending the property after personally inspecting over 50 properties in the last 12 months.'

At that meeting it was agreed to go ahead with the purchase subject to a satisfactory surveyor's report and, on 1st July 1975 contracts were exchanged. The price for the two properties was £95,000.

One Crusader who was more than a little interested in the purchase was our Solicitor, Mr Derek Warren, for as a small boy he had joined the St Albans Crusader Class under the leadership of 'Bubbly' alias Lawrence C Head which in those days met, guess where? Yes, in the Abbey Institute! Crusaders were coming home to roost!

The change in the location of Headquarters was by no means the only change being envisaged in 1975. Mary Bevington and I were both approaching the age when men and women are expected to retire unless you are a judge or a President of the United States and so in the September we bade farewell to Mary.

She will be remembered by many, not only because she was the first paid Secretary appointed to administer the girls' side of the work, but also for all she did during her fifteen years in office in helping to lay foundations in the early vital formative years of the Crusaders Union Girls' Association, together with her care and concern for a satisfactory integration as the two sides of the movement began gradually to come together.

Heather Keep, appointed CUGA General Secretary in 1975, now Assistant Director

Happily Mary had on her staff one whose competence, experience and character made her the ideal successor. A Crusader in her teens and then a leader at Whetstone, Heather Keep had left the teaching profession to join Mary as Assistant Secretary and over the years had endeared herself to all who knew her. She accepted the position of General Secretary with some hesitation at first, typical of her, but the passing years clearly proved the GA Committee's wisdom in making the appointment.

Another excellent decision about this time was the appointment of Pam McKellen to take over Heather's responsibilities as Assistant Secretary – another teacher who had been Housemistress at a Manchester school and a Leader of the Sale Class. She was soon putting her gifts to good use particularly in the administration of the Camps and Houseparties.

It was now twenty years since the boys' Union had taken under its wing a group of lady leaders who had decided to withdraw from the Girl Crusaders' Union, regarding it as a temporary measure until their problems had been satisfactorily resolved and the status quo restored. Unfortunately, as already related, every endeavour to reach a solution acceptable to all concerned had failed, and ultimately, for the sake of the Classes involved it had seemed desirable to put the girls' work on a proper basis, and so the Crusaders' Union Girls' Association had been formed, even though the General Committee went on hoping for a satisfactory solution; they genuinely didn't want what most regarded as the complication and distraction of a girls' work permanently on their hands!

But the girls' work grew and went on growing, new Classes were started and in due course someone somewhere even mentioned the idea of a mixed Class! Like Queen Victoria of old, the boys' Leaders generally 'were not amused' at this revolutionary suggestion!

However as year succeeded year the inevitable evolutionary process went on quietly and gently until what had once seemed almost unthinkable began to be regarded as at least a possibility, and finally it seemed positively unreasonable to regard the CUGA as a kind of subsidiary movement, with every decision of the ladies' Committee subject to confirmation by the boys' General Committee.

At first the two Committees began to meet occasionally in joint session; then this became every other month, and finally at a Special Business Meeting on 10th February 1976 the CU Leaders adopted a new Constitution which had the effect of making the two movements one. What had at first seemed a tragedy had, in fact, become a blessing in disguise for without seeking it, we now had a movement more suited to the tremendous social changes which had taken place in the nation at large, and Crusader Classes now had the facility to be, or to become, mixed if the local situation made this desirable.

In my final report to the leadership presented at the Annual Business Meeting on 22nd May 1976, I recall writing the following:

'We shall all join in remembering often, at the Throne of Grace, the men and women who are now responsible for the government of the Union, as a fresh chapter in its history is opened at a time when Britain generally has lost its faith and has consequently lost its way.'

And now what about my successor when I retired in February 1976? The position of Secretary and Treasurer in the branch of the Union in Scotland had always been an Honorary appointment first held by John Eaton and then for many years by Norman Wright, followed later by Bill Crawford and Walter Ritchie. Next came a Leader of the Bearsden Class named Melville Paton who had trained and was practising as a civil engineer in Glasgow. Having occupied the position of Secretary and Treasurer in an honorary capacity, he offered to devote two years working full-time for Crusaders in Scotland, a generous and most welcome gesture.

I well recall meeting Melville Paton in his office at 280 St Vincent Street, Glasgow, and being impressed by his business-like efficiency and his deep devotion to the work of the Union, North of the Border. It crossed my mind

New Headquarters in the shadow of St Albans Abbey

The Book Centre

at the time that perhaps here was the one to take my place when the time came. I shared my thoughts with the General Committee and so it was that in due course Melville accepted their invitation to be my successor.

It was decided we should work together during my final months so that he could familiarise himself with all that went on at Headquarters. It was during this time we acquired the St Albans property and it would be hard to over-estimate the value of Melville's engineering skill and know-how, for he was able to keep an eye on the gutting, refurbishing and adaptation of both No 2 Romeland Hill and of Tankerfield House next door. His supervising and discerning watchfulness as the work proceeded was invaluable.

Incidentally we discovered with interest that Tankerfield House was so named after the man who, close by, was burnt at the stake because of his unwillingness to renounce his Christian faith; clearly we were to occupy holy ground.

The records have reminded me that at the time we had the sum of £117,259 in the Appeal Fund, of which £22,635 comprised interest free loans, and happily enough our application for 'Improvement Grants' was regarded favourably by the local Council and we received the welcome sum of £3,200 in respect of the two flats in Tankerville House. In due course Melville moved in to one of these flats and Robin Croxon and his wife - he worked in the Bookshop - moved into the other.

When the work of reconstruction and adaptation was finished we had a perfect Headquarters in a delightful situation in the shadow of the Abbey, and no more worries about paying rent. An added bonus was that we were now nearer to our Camp Equipment store at Piccots End, Hemel Hempstead, where for many years, Dennis Lowden (ex Golders Green Class) ably supported by Elizabeth his wife, cared for, repaired, replaced, issued, received back and restored all our camping equipment; a labour of love if ever there was one. It meant that all our camps were always provided with equipment in first class condition, an invaluable asset when living under canvas.

When the move from Ludgate Hill eventually took place in September 1976, all members of the staff found themselves able to reach St Albans without difficulty each day - with two exceptions. David Gregory had joined us as a school-leaver and throughout the following seventeen years had made himself thoroughly conversant with the book trade, and his zeal to make the most of the Union's Bookroom never waned. Family circumstances made it impossible for him to move house and Billericay in Essex was much too far from St Albans to justify commuting. His loyal service is remembered with gratitude. Jane Robertson who had given invaluable help as a Secretary in the Camps work was also unable to manage the long journey from Dartford.

The only other member of staff faced with a sizeable journey was Ray Allison but the daily drive from Buckhurst Hill presented no problems to this Jehu! It would be hard to over-value Ray's service to Headquarters although his somewhat nonchalant manner tends to disguise his ability to organise and, equally important, his facility with figures - and now with computers. Leader of a flourishing Class, Ray joined us initially as the organiser of Camps and Houseparties, but when Dan Mahony retired, Ray became Business Manager. To have a Chartered Accountant in the Headquarters team was a luxury indeed, but a very precious one, for we always knew exactly where we were as the Union's finances and accounting machinery became more complex.

After a time Pam decided to live in St Albans and so too did Jenny Haddon, who was a faithful member of staff for many years and whose loving, gentle nature, coupled with a keen sense of humour, was a real asset to Headquarters, quite apart from her ability and efficiency in all she did.

The members of the Staff were soon happily settled into their new Headquarters and they quickly discovered its many benefits; quite apart from the excellent facilities inside, the location provided a most attractive environment. Fresh air and quietness had replaced the noise and the fume-laden atmosphere of Ludgate Hill, while green fields close by had replaced the concrete jungle around St Pauls, and shopping in the lunch hour in St Albans was infinitely superior to shopping in Paternoster Square.

It felt like a new beginning, and in several respects it was, for, as already mentioned the newly adopted Constitution had effected a marriage between the two sides of the movement and now the General Committee comprised both men and women equally responsible for the management of the Union. At their meeting in September 1976 it was decided that Melville Paton should be General Secretary and Heather Keep Joint General Secretary, so both sides of the work could be suitably watched over and developed.

It had been agreed several months previously that, when all was ready, a service of Thanksgiving and Dedication of the new Headquarters should be arranged. In due course the Dean of St Albans, the Very Reverend Peter Moore was approached; he warmly welcomed the request for the service to take place in the Cathedral and readily agreed to take part which included the formal handing over of the Deeds of the Abbey Institute and Tankerville House.

And so on Saturday, 23rd October 1976, the Cathedral was filled with Crusaders for an inspiring service which will long be remembered by those present, after which Sir Eric Richardson, as President of the Union, unveiled a plaque in the wall of the new Headquarters to mark the occasion.

Later at a reception, Russell Warner, the Committee Chairman, thanked the Dean for his warm-hearted co-operation. In reply the Dean said how glad he was that the Union had purchased the Institute building and how happy he was that the dedication had taken place in the Abbey. I well recall his final words: "The Abbey is yours" and with a smile and as an afterthought "not yours to flog, of course!" His genuine friendliness and that of many of the workers in the Abbey has been a greatly appreciated asset, so too has their Refectory which provides excellent meals at very reasonable prices!

By the week leading up to the Thanksgiving Service all the money needed for the new building had been received in gifts or interest free loans - a wonderful confirmation that it was God's place for the new Headquarters.

When in due course John Taylor became Bishop of St Albans, our link was even stronger for, when a boy, he had been a member of the Crusader Class in Watford and gladly testifies to the help and blessing it had been to him in his formative years. When he later appointed Ken Pillar as his Suffragan Bishop of Hertford we had yet another Crusader link living down the lane close by. Ken had been a Plymouth Crusader and he will be particularly remembered by many who in earlier days had visited the Lee Abbey Conference Centre, near Lynton in Devon, where, for several years, he was the much-loved Warden.

John Taylor, Bishop of St Albans and one-time Watford Crusader

25

ALL CHANGE

Since my retirement in 1976 I have watched with interest the many changes taking place in Crusaders; changes which have been essential because of the rapidly changing situation in our land.

Perhaps the most significant change affecting Crusaders from the mid 60s onwards was the introduction of comprehensive education. The main catchment area of the movement had long been the grammar and public schools. With the introduction of the all-ability policy of State schools, this group of young people was no longer separated off by the education system and friends were made right across the spectrum of academic abilities and social class. This was probably one of the main causes for the beginning of a decline in the boys' membership from the late 60s.

During the 70s and into the early 80s there was continued steady decline in numbers and considerable time was spent on Committee considering the way forward. At the leaders' conference at Swanwick in 1982 Dr Robert Hunt, then Chairman of the General Committee, presented a paper entitled 'The Future of Crusaders' which included an analysis of statistics and a review of the problems facing the movement. He faced the questions posed by declining membership and discussed their possible implications. Had Crusaders fulfilled its purpose or were there still clear indications that the work should continue?

Looking at the available active human resources in devoted Christian leadership throughout the movement, together with the experience and expertise in youth work this represented, Robert Hunt and Committee firmly believed there was excellent justification for pressing on, while adapting Crusaders to a changed and changing situation in the nation at large. A belief shared strongly by the leaders at the conference where the mood was upbeat, positive and encouraging.

In point of fact, new ideas were already being tried; for example, while many Classes were still following the traditional Sunday afternoon pattern of Bible Class, others had abandoned this format for a less formal midweek evening programme, while others had moved still further to a complete 'club night' pattern with games, competitions and all the normal club night items, but always with a time set aside for spiritual matters. It was a case of 'by all means'. Nearly all new Classes elected were mixed and a number of the existing separate boys' and girls' Classes had merged. A further change was that several Classes had opened which were church-linked, following a number of enquiries from churches who felt it would help their youth out-reach work to be part of Crusaders.

At the end of 1981 Melville Paton returned to Christian work in Scotland and Heather acted as General Secretary while very careful consideration was given to the best way forward for the general administration and future staff structure of the work. After much prayerful thought, Committee felt that the time had come to appoint a Director, instead of a General Secretary; this role would allow the person appointed more freedom to give a strong lead to the work, though he would still be responsible to the General Committee. So the post was advertised.

It came as a surprise to many leaders when eventually it was announced that someone named Ernie Addicott had been appointed, someone completely unknown to Crusaders and who had had very little previous connection with the movement. When leaders first met him, they were even more surprised. Had a film producer required someone suitable to play the part of a swash-buckling pilot in the war-time RAF, he would have needed to look no further; Ernie had it all, complete with a fiercesome-looking handlebar moustache! Anyone reading these words who actually served in the RAF during the war, would have been reminded of Pilot Officer Prune in the magazine TM. What was even more surprising, Ernie had been a post-war test pilot at the Royal Aircraft Establishment at Farnborough, but had recently returned from Africa after serving as a pilot with the Missionary Aviation Fellowship.

Ernie came into the work in April 1983 but had been able to attend the Swanwick Conference in the previous October. He was completely free from any inhibitions from the past in Crusaders and as he began to grasp the situation, he expressed himself as follows:

'The challenge, clearly was to channel the energy and creativity which I saw in Crusaders without smothering the flexibility of approach and the strong-willed individuality of so many gifted leaders. It seemed to me the answer must lie in seeking the common elements in our vision as a movement and presenting it in some kind of corporate plan which could take Crusaders forward into the next decade and beyond.'

With this in mind, he felt the need to consult the leadership at large in order to ascertain and confirm the movement's calling, and how best to respond to it in the current circumstances. A video entitled 'Crusaders, on the Right Road?' was produced for members of the Headquarters' Staff to take to a series of leaders' regional meetings to gather reaction and feedback. It focused attention on the encouraging aspects of the movement, and sought to promote discussion on what needed to be done to ensure a viable future.

The response to the meetings was mixed, but it was very helpful to meet leaders and to get their feedback. The gathering in the Refectory of St Albans Abbey was particularly encouraging, '...vision and enthusiasm predominated and there was a great sense of God's presence'.

One of the lessons learned by those involved in the regional gatherings was the need to raise the profile of Crusaders, and in an effort to deal with this Ernie decided to become involved with Spring Harvest at Prestatyn. After a few days there he became very disappointed for, although usefully involved in counselling, nothing had occurred so far as making contacts for Crusaders was concerned. Late one evening, almost with a feeling of desperation, he prayed for some confirmation regarding his purpose for being there at all. He asked for just one contact, and now in his own words:

'Early next morning I headed for the exhibition hall on my way to the prayer meeting and stopped by the pigeonhole where messages were left for exhibition representatives. I was quite staggered! There in my pigeonhole was a message asking me to contact someone to discuss the possibility of starting a new Crusader group.'

Nor was that all, for before the end of the week he had made contact with six young students eager to help in a Crusader group near their college. It served to provide the encouragement he was needing.

A very significant development took place in 1985. Ken Morgan, a leader at Virginia Water Crusaders, had by then succeeded Robert Hunt as Chairman. While on a visit to the United States he had seen something of the work of 'Young Life' and at one Committee Meeting suggested that what Crusaders needed was 'field-workers' in various areas of the country to look for new leaders and help plant new groups. This was a marvellous concept but could Crusaders take on a number of extra paid workers?

Then Arnie Jacobs, a retired worker from 'Young Life' visited Headquarters and again stressed the value of field-workers. In fact, he could not understand how any movement could function successfully with only an administrative staff and all else performed on a voluntary basis! Was this an indication of the 'right road' ahead? Clearly the leadership must be consulted once again and so it was that in September 1985 a day conference for area representatives was arranged to discuss the idea of appointing a 'Development Worker'.

Ernie Addicott, Director 1983-1992

A CRUSOE Project in Bolivia

A South London Development Worker with some members of a new group at Amott Road Baptist Church in Peckham

A Development Worker shares God's Word

On a Leadership Training Course –
active teaching!

On a
Crusader
Holiday

Alan Kerbey, Director 1992-

Crusaders Today

The day was attended by people from every Crusader Area including Scotland and Northern Ireland. At the end of the meeting there was total agreement to adopt the policy of employing full-time Development Workers with the result that, soon afterwards, Alan Dodds was appointed to East Anglia. He was a Church Army Captain and had been working as Training Director with British Youth For Christ.

At the Swanwick conference in 1986, Alan Dodds reported on his first year's experience as a Crusader Development Worker. To quote Ernie Addicott:

'The conference was visibly excited by his electrifying account of how the Lord had opened up the way for planting a spectacular eleven new groups, four of them already open and functioning; the others well-advanced in their preparations to start. Clearly the 'pilot project' had made an excellent start.'

Soon further Development Workers were appointed and today many Areas of the country have their own Worker; all the appointments being made on the basis of the Area finding the support for the Worker. John Eakins in Sussex and Portsdown was one of the first to be appointed and now leads the team of Development Workers.

God had clearly led over this historic development. Since 1986 Crusaders' overall membership has been slowly increasing, and 1991, 1992 and 1993 saw all-time records in the number of new groups (as classes are now called) elected.

There were a number of other important changes during these years. In the early 80s plans were drawn up for a revision of the Crusader Constitution with a view to replacing the General Committee and General Purposes Sub-Committee with a Council and an Executive Committee. The Council would be large, with representatives from every Crusader Area and would meet only three times a year; the Executive would be elected annually by the Council and would meet monthly to provide a short-term decision making mechanism and oversight of the implementation of Council policy. The new Constitution was adopted by the Annual Business Meeting in May 1983 and the new system proved to be very effective.

Crusader Holidays continued to be a blessing to hundreds of young people each year. Pam McKellen and the Holidays Sub-Committee worked hard to provide a programme to meet changing demands: new sites, new activities and a gradual swing from separate boys' and girls' holidays to a majority of mixed holidays. A further change was to advertise the Holidays in various Christian magazines with the result that increasing numbers of non-Crusaders began to benefit from them. With more and more Area and group Holidays being arranged, the number of Crusaders at the national holidays was declining and the move to invite non-Crusaders helped to make a viable programme.

Taking on board the feedback from the video 'Crusaders, on the Right Road?', the many conversations he had had with leaders, and research into the youth scene and the social environment in which Crusaders was operating, Ernie drew up a five-year Strategic Plan for Crusaders (1986-1991), 'Advancing into the Nineties'. One of the major conclusions from his research into Christian youth work generally was that the vast majority of workers was concentrating on the small minority of less than 10% of young people who were involved in one way or another with a church. Others were concerned to reach the very needy young people who were into drugs and serious crime, but the broad middle irreligious and unchurched band of youngsters was largely untouched. The Plan emphasised that this 80% or so needed to be Crusaders' target group and a set of initiatives were proposed to move Crusaders closer to reaching this group.

Many leaders were not used to dealing with totally unchurched young people and it was recognised that there would need to be great emphasis on equipping and training leaders for this task, both existing leaders and the many new leaders it was believed would be coming into the work. For some years, Brenda Cuthbert from Dunchurch Crusaders had been very involved in Crusaders' Leadership Training and in 1985 she joined the Staff team in a part-time capacity as Leadership Training Co-ordinator and a year later was appointed full-time. Her energy and creative ideas brought great sparkle to the training programme and Leadership Training began to take on increasing importance at every level.

During these years Crusaders international links were developing in an exciting way too. As a result of Ernie Addicott's vision and energy, CRUSOE, CRUSaders Overseas Expeditions, was launched in 1986 with a work project in Tanzania to help villagers to extend two airstrips. This project, and an increasing number which have taken place in following years, proved to be a life-changing experience for many Crusaders of 16 years and over: three or four weeks in the summer spent in Africa, South America, India or Eastern Europe, giving an opportunity to sample short-term service abroad.

One of the proposals in the Strategic Plan was to raise the profile of Crusaders and, on the advice of a Christian advertising agency, it was decided to bring out a high quality magazine once a term to replace some of the in-house mailings; a magazine which would be suitable for leaders, associates and students. In September 1986 'LINK' magazine was born and was soon widely appreciated. Heather Keep, who had become Assistant Director on Ernie's appointment, took on the editorship.

The Plan also proposed appointing a full-time person to look after Public Relations in Crusaders and in September 1990 this possibility was met most acceptably in the appointment of Olaf Fogwill, who had been a lecturer in marketing, and who rejoiced at the opportunity to use his undoubted gifts in so worthwhile a spiritual project among young people.

One of the many assets of the move of Headquarters to St Albans was having space for a well-stocked Book Centre on the ground floor. Here Guy Marshall, who became Book Centre Manager in 1982, and his staff provide a valuable service both to Crusaders and the general public.

The Book Centre stocks a great range of teaching resources but the need for materials for leaders reaching out to completely unchurched youngsters was becoming more and more apparent. From the early 80s occasional teaching projects were produced from Head Office, as Headquarters came to be called, but there was a need for much more material. God's provision for this need was seen when in 1992 Elaine Williams joined the Staff as Teaching Resources Co-ordinator: her experience as a Leader at Letchworth and as a secondary school teacher helped to make her the ideal choice for this post.

In recording some of this most recent history of Crusaders, I have made free use of a treatise which Ernie Addicott kindly prepared at my request. I cannot do better than quote verbatim from his final paragraph in which he says:

'God called Crusaders to a very specific task way back at the turn of the Century. That task was to introduce young people who were out of ear-shot of the Church to a personal relationship with Jesus, prepare them for responsible Christian living and integrate them into an adult Christian fellowhip.

The social grouping most at risk of missing out on the Gospel has changed. Young people's culture and interests have changed considerably. Teaching and communication methods have changed most dramatically of all, but Crusaders' calling has not changed in the least.

Indeed, since the mid-eighties, I believe we have seen that calling renewed with fresh urgency and fresh anointing. We have the great privilege of being a part of something powerful and beautiful that God is doing among us and through us. We can but walk with Him and obey His voice as He moves us in new directions and into new fields of opportunity. He has been faithful in the past. We can trust Him for all that's to come.'

To which we can all add a heartfelt "Amen", at the same time paying a sincere tribute of gratitude for Ernie's nine years of service to Crusaders. It came as a great surprise when he announced his intention to resign at a time when the situation was so encouraging, but he was sure that it was God's timing.

So it was that in August 1992, Dr Alan Kerbey became the new Director: a research scientist from Oxford University who had done much valuable work in respect of the treatment of diabetes. It would be hard to find a character so completely different from that of his predecessor. Ernie's flamboyance had been replaced by a quiet, gentle, winsome personality. One whose experience as a researcher should prove invaluable in exploring and assessing what aspects of the movement in today's situation are worthy of encouragement and development. It all seems completely appropriate for such a fluid time as this and so, once again, we can say with heartfelt gratitude, "Hitherto has the Lord helped us".

In the year 1900, God did a new thing to help meet a changing situation; at the time no-one could have guessed that the result would be thousands of young folk brought to faith in Christ and to devoted Christian discipleship. Today we are confronted by a situation among young people far more serious and challenging than that faced by our forefathers. Then it was mainly a question of boredom but not unbelief in Christianity, which was generally accepted as a normal ingredient of British life.

Now, to many of our citizens, God does not exist and the Christian religion is a mere relic of the past, with the resultant disintegration of the moral and ethical fabric of the nation. All this is taking place against a backdrop of distress and disaster in so many parts of the world, and almost every news bulletin tells of war, famine and murder.

I am reminded of a speech by Sir Winston Churchill when he was awarded the Nobel Peace Prize, in which he said:

'Since Alfred Nobel died in 1896, we have entered an age of storm and tragedy. The power of man has grown in every sphere, except over himself... the fearful question confronts us: have our problems got beyond our control? Undoubtedly we are passing through a phase when this may be so. Well may we humble ourselves and seek for guidance and mercy.'

Looking at Britain today through the medium of television and the press, we seem to have become a people enslaved by materialism, sex and violence. No evening programme on TV appears complete without a shameless demonstration of it. Jesus said, "Whatsoever a man sows that shall he also reap" and we are now seeing the inevitable harvest. It is no longer safe for children to walk alone to and from school. During the war, in winter everyone walked about in complete darkness and we were perfectly safe – except for German bombs! Now, if having to walk alone at night, one is relieved to arrive home safely. What of the future? I recall the title of a book which may well indicate the answer, it was 'Creed or Chaos'.

On one of the many occasions when Israel 'did evil in the sight of the Lord', God allowed them to be taken captive to Babylon. With Jerusalem devastated and their Temple destroyed, the Jews might well have lost all hope in their future as God's chosen people. But a small group, with the fire of faith still burning, were allowed by Darius the king to return to Jerusalem, their aim to rebuild the Temple, to have God back at the centre of their homeland. As the building began to take shape, some older members of the party became thoroughly disheartened as they remembered the grandeur and glory of the old Temple. Haggai records:

'Who is left among you that saw this house in its former glory? How do you see it now? Is it not in your sight as nothing? Yet now take courage, O Zerubbabel... for I am with you says the Lord of hosts... My Spirit abides among you; fear not... the latter splendour of this house shall be greater than the former.'

The more I have pondered this passage, the more it seems to reflect our situation today for we are witnessing Crusaders, as a movement, being rebuilt under completely different circumstances and conditions. Inevitably there will be some among us who remember the days gone by when hundreds of girls and boys arrived at their various meeting places with their Bibles tucked under their arms, and looking forward with happy expectation to all that was meant by the words 'Crusaders' Bible Class'.

Our nostalgic thoughts and comparisons can be forgiven but realism must over-ride regrets as we give what support we can to encourage the builders of today. Their aim is just the same, to introduce young folk to the Saviour by sowing the good seed of God's word in their minds and hearts, knowing that 'faith comes by hearing and hearing by the word of God', always remembering that only the Spirit of God can give life to the seed. The vital significance of this was re-emphasised to those Jewish builders of the Temple only a few months after God had assured them through Haggai that 'My Spirit abides among you' for along comes an angel to tell Zechariah, "This is the word of the Lord to Zerubbabel: 'Not by might, not by power, but by my Spirit says the Lord Almighty'."

The new 'building' now taking shape will often be very different from its predecessor. 'Club night' may have replaced 'Bible Class', but the object has not changed. To emphasise this I am reminded of a book by a Bishop of Sheffield entitled: 'The Seed and the Fruit', an extract of which reads as follows:

'As the threats of war and the cries of the dispossessed were sounding in his ears, Western Man fell into an uneasy sleep. In his sleep he dreamed that he entered the spacious store in which the gifts of God to men are kept, and addressed the angel behind the counter, saying: "I have run out of the fruits of the Spirit, can you restock me?" When the angel seemed about to say no, he burst out, "In place of war, afflictions, injustice, lying and lust, I need love, joy, peace, integrity, discipline. Without these I shall be lost." And the angel behind the counter replied, "We do not stock fruit - only seeds".'

For more than 90 years, Crusader leaders have seen again and again what can happen when God's word is prayerfully, carefully and patiently taught to boys and girls. Gradually many discover for themselves the reality and wonder of God's love for them in Christ, the joy of sins forgiven, and the promise of His presence and guidance as they begin to face the challenge of life's uncertain future: 'Looking unto Jesus' - 'the same yesterday and today and forever'.

This stylised version of the badge was introduced in the 80's to give a more modern image and the logo incorporating it in the early 90's. The original badge is still used as the presentation one after 10 attendances.